# WITH THE TURK IN WARTIME

# WITH THE TURK IN WARTIME

## MARMADUKE PICKTHALL

1 2 3 4 5 6 7 8 9 10

CLARITAS BOOKS

Bernard Street, Swansea, United Kingdom
Milpitas, California, United States

© CLARITAS BOOKS 2018

This book is in copyright. Subject to statutory exception and to the provisions of relevant collective licensing agreements, no reproduction of any part may take place without the written permission of Claritas Books.

First Published in June 2018

Typeset in Minion Pro

With The Turk in Wartime
By Marmaduke Pickthall

A CIP catalogue record for this book is available from the British Library

ISBN: 978-1-905837-58-8

**Marmaduke Pickthall** was a Western Islamic scholar noted for his English translation of the Quran. A convert from Christianity, Pickthall was a novelist, esteemed by D. H. Lawrence, H. G. Wells, and E. M. Forster, as well as a journalist, headmaster, and political and religious leader. As a schoolboy at Harrow School, Pickthall was a classmate and friend of Winston Churchill. Pickthall travelled across many Eastern countries. Before declaring his faith as a Muslim, Pickthall was a strong ally of the Ottoman Empire. He studied the Orient, and published articles and novels on the subject. While in the service of the Nizam of Hyderabad, Pickthall published his English translation of the Quran with the title '*The Meaning of the Glorious Quran*'. The translation was authorised by the Al-Azhar University in Egypt. Pickthall died in 1936 and buried in the Muslim section at Brookwood Cemetery in Surrey, England, where Abdullah Yusuf Ali was later buried.

# CONTENTS

INTRODUCTION                              11

CHAPTER I: Arrival                        15

CHAPTER II: Stamboul and Pera             23

CHAPTER III: House Hunting                31

CHAPTER IV: Pinetree Kiosk                39

CHAPTER V: The Neighbours                 47

CHAPTER VI: Views of England              55

CHAPTER VII: A Garden Party               63

CHAPTER VIII: A Modern Khoja              71

CHAPTER IX: Ottoman Greeks                79

CHAPTER XI: The Woman Question            87

CHAPTER XI: Political Gossip              99

CHAPTER XII: A Conspirator                107

**CHAPTER XIII:** The Eleventh of June 115

**CHAPTER XIV:** Assassination as a Tonic 123

**CHAPTER XV:** The Men and the Cause of the Conspiracy 129

**CHAPTER XVI:** The Army of the West 137

**CHAPTER XVII:** The Season of the Fires 143

**CHAPTER XVIII:** Ottoman Education 149

**CHAPTER XIX:** Cosmopolitan Education 155

**CHAPTER XX:** Checks on Progress 161

**CHAPTER XXI:** Islam and Progress 167

**CHAPTER XXII:** Farewells 175

# INTRODUCTION

In February of the year 1913 I made up my mind to go to Turkey for a few months in order to escape an atmosphere which sickened me. The English Press and public had, in this twentieth century, responded with fanaticism to the cry of a Crusade against the Turk raised by some cunning Balkan rulers; and that fanaticism had been fostered, as it seemed to my intelligence, by British statesmen — not for their country's ends, but for the ends and in the interests of Russia, our great Eastern rival. The solidarity of Christendom against a Muslim power was reckoned a fine thing by many people; but it broke the heart of Englishmen who loved the East. For what had England stood for until then, in India and throughout her Eastern empire? Had she not stood for universal toleration, for a nationality which should be independent of religious differences? The Turks of their own will espoused the same ideal; since when they had been plundered and attacked on all hands. And what had England done but smile upon their persecutors?

"The Concert of the Powers", "The Peace of Europe" must be preserved at all costs, we were told: even at the cost — a slight one, in the view of politicians — of national prestige and honour. Oh, Europe! Europe! Is it all the world? Nobody thought of Asia looking on. And if one mentioned it, he was informed that Asia did not count, being uncivilised and, what appeared to many a conclusive argument, outside the pale of Christianity. It seemed to me that there were two kinds of Christianity: one, which would limit its benevolence to Christian peoples; the other, which regarded the world with all its creeds and races as the theatre for Christian charity and Christian justice. The first, which still prevailed in Russia and the Balkan states, and still could claim adherents here in England, was essentially the same fanaticism which we blame so loudly when it appears in the more ignorant Muslims. The second gave the spirit of our Eastern empire, the spirit of humanity and tolerance which one associates with modern life. If we (England) discarded the second and embraced the first — though only in appearance, and from motives of high policy concerned with Russia — the literal minded East, observant of our conduct step by step, would call us liars; we should have betrayed the faith which they had placed in us, and forfeited all moral claim to their allegiance. There was, besides, another aspect of the case. The East was waking; though the bulk of it lay still unconscious, wrapped in its traditions like our medieval forbears. It had been my lot in early youth to be immersed in the unconsciousness of the old East, to receive its spirit for a season and to know its charm. Since then I had observed, with some annoyance, the various attacks of conscious Europe on unconscious Asia, and the stirring of the latter towards a consciousness akin to ours. It had been strange to see the men responsible for that awakening shrink back in horror as did Frankenstein before his monster, trying frantically but in vain to wreck their work. To me it seemed unreason near to madness for us English even to attempt to stop a movement which owed its inspiration largely to the work of Englishmen and English governments; and such attempts, I thought, would certainly entail a heavy penalty. The conscious nations, striving selfishly for their own ends failed altogether to remark the obvious historic truth: that it was the thing they strove not for that came to pass inevitably; in other words, that a natural Nemesis attended brutal egotism in the world of nations as surely as in that of individuals; again, in other words, that God exists. Because the penalty was not immediate, it was disregarded by our politicians; but such short-sightedness in men paid and appointed to see well and far, deserved the nation's censure. Turkey, a country in close touch with Europe, was the head of the progressive movement in the East, the natural head, the sanest head that could be chosen; for the Turk was capable of understanding Europe and acting as interpreter to those behind him. If we cut off that head, as Russia, our ally, and other Powers desired to do, a hundred mad fanatic heads would rise instead of it, a monster would be formed which would devour our children. Or so it seemed to me when I set out for Turkey, nor have I since seen anything to change my view. People in a position to be well informed, assured me I was altogether wrong, because the Turks were hopelessly demoralised, the revolution had turned out a ghastly failure, and so on. They told me to go to Constantinople and see for myself. I had not been there for some eighteen years; my more recent knowledge of the Ottoman Empire, intimate though it was, being practically restricted to the Arab provinces. I had, therefore, no reply to make to such opponents, though I knew their judgment faulty, except to take their advice and go and judge for myself. Accordingly, having been well supplied with introductions by the kindness of some friends, I set out to investigate the state of Turkey, as far as might be, from a Turkish point of view. The results of that investigation may be gathered from this little work, which first appeared as a series of articles in the New Age. In it I have endeavoured to portray the state of things which I beheld, both good and evil, fairly, hiding nothing. For obvious reasons I have altered or suppressed the names of my associates. I have also, here and there, condensed a conversation, or merged a number of occasions into one; and, leaving out the usual tourist business of description, I have treated mainly of the things which struck me as significant. Apart from this the narrative is unembellished. I hope that it will not be found uninteresting.

## CHAPTER I
# ARRIVAL

We were on the Black Sea, but our eyes looked out on something absolutely colourless. All view was curtained off from us by fog — a fog as thick as cotton-wool, by which the steamer's length was partly hidden. Because of this our ship was hardly going, its progress being governed by the movements of a row-boat on ahead, of which the occupants were taking soundings. We heard them shouting numbers in Romanian close to us, but could not see a shadow of the boat or them. And ever and anon the fog-horn deafened us. Once we were very nearly on some rocks, a fellow-passenger informed me; once I myself was witness of the near escape we had of a collision with another steamer. There were despairing shouts as the vague shapes of funnels and a hull loomed out before us suddenly, right in our course, and very close indeed. The sudden backing of the engines made us reel. It was after that escape that we began to go so slowly and the rowing-boat was sent ahead to clear the way. There were about forty other passengers on board, none of them English. At that time people shunned Constantinople on account of the war, the alleged instability of the Government, and the reported danger of a massacre of Europeans. Having come from Berlin — which was pro-Turk territory — and not from Paris, I had not heard the dreadful rumours which disturbed the minds of several of my fellow-travellers; and, hearing them, could laugh at their improbability. One French lady, hysterically anxious to rejoin her husband who had some employment in the threatened city, repeatedly bemoaned her case to an acquaintance that she had on board, seeming to think the fog of evil omen for her husband's fate. All the Europeans seemed put out and anxious, impatient of delay; but the Turks, of whom there were a few among us, were resigned, as usual, and I, who had no pressing claim on time, was able to assume and feel the same indifference. At evening it became known that we had missed the entrance to the Bosphorus and, even should we afterwards succeed in striking it, could not go in now as it was past six o'clock. The ship dropped anchor; then madame began to sob aloud, and exclamations of annoyance came from all sides. We should have to spend forty-eight hours upon a passage which was commonly performed in twelve. It was disgusting, quite insufferable! One gentleman — a Greek — professing to know exactly where we were, suggested we should launch the boats and row ashore to Rumeli Cavak, whence we could take a Bosphorus steamer to Constantinople. His notion found no favour with the rest of us. If the skipper and the pilot could not find the way, we thought it little likely that a landsman would be more successful. Besides, the fog was deadly cold, the visible small patch of sea dark and repellent in its smoothness like thin ice. There was warmth and comfort and good food on board the steamer, and everyone at length agreed to make the best of it. A sense of kinship in adversity was born in us, and that night everybody talked to everybody. One plunged at once to friendship without the usual fence of

## Chapter I Arrival

courtesies. One man told me the whole history of his married life — he never knew my name, nor I his — and showed me photographs to illustrate it, in the dining-room; another tucked his arm in mine affectionately, and asked my help to send a wireless telegram. After dinner I put on an overcoat, turned up the collar, and went out on deck to smoke alone. The fog was still as thick as ever. Our siren and the big horn spoke at intervals; and from the darkness upon all sides other hoots and shrieks responded, from sea-waifs anchored round us in the fog. I soon got to know their several voices and look out for them, and conceived some notion of their bearings in respect of us. As I was strolling up and down on deck a man approached, whom I had remarked by day for his obsequious adherence to the first-class passengers, though he himself was of the second class. He passed me with a conscious little smile — in doubt, it seemed, whether to speak or no. I did not look forbidding, evidently, for a minute later, as I stood beside the rail, staring point-blank at nothing, trying to locate the different fog-horns which kept sounding in that black consistency, he was at my side, addressing me in French of the Byzantine school, observing it was cold, extremely — very, very cold. I made polite rejoinder.

He exclaimed, "Ah, you are French?"

"No," I said; and then, as he appeared consumed with eagerness to know my nationality, reluctantly confessed that I was English. It seemed a shame to make no more exciting statement, in view of his inquiring zeal.

"Ah," he replied, "I thought you must be English by your pipe and the fashion of your overcoat. There is an air about the English which the other nations lack entirely. I am very happy to make your acquaintance. We love the English much. If you desire it, I can speak English with you." To show his powers in this direction, he added, "How do you do, sir?" in my native tongue. But as I took no notice of the interjection, the conversation was pursued in French.

"Where are you going?"
"To Constantinople."
"Have you been there before?"
"Once. It must be eighteen years ago."
"What is your business there?"
"I have no business there. I go for pleasure."
"For pleasure — in this time of war, and in the winter! That is little probable."

My inquisitor now smiled, incredulous. In talking, we had turned so as to face each other, each leaning with one elbow on the rail. The light of a near lamp was on his face, a sleek one and a fatuous, to me displeasing. He wore a fez, but was no Turk; the fact was patent from his impudence. "Perhaps," he said, exceeding knowingly, "you have some secret mission which you will not tell me." To slay this notion, which, if spread abroad among the vulgar, might well have gained me undeserved and undesired attentions, I informed him of the truth: that I was going to Constantinople simply to observe the state of things in Turkey.

"Ah, then, you are a politician?"
"No; a writer."
"Ah, it is very fortunate that I have met you. I can tell you everything. Are there any questions you would like to ask me? I am well informed of everything in Turkey. I have secret informations which I can procure for you."

I put a question as to the atrocities committed by the Bulgarians in Macedonia. This made him snigger.

"That is all a fabrication. I have private information from a friend of mine at Dedeagach, where the Turks have slaughtered all the Christians."

It so happened that Dedeagach was one of the very few places where we had respectable European evidence upon the horrors committed by Bulgarian troops and Komitadjis. I said as much. At once my friend revoked, exclaiming:

"I will tell you how it was. The Turks began to massacre,

killing two or three; so the Bulgars said: You will either become Christians or leave the country, or else we will massacre you all. Were they not right? Ah, sir, you do not know all that we have to suffer, we Christians here in Turkey, from the fanaticism of the Muslims. I shall be happy to inform you fully. I am at your disposal."

I smoked in silence for a while before replying:

"You talk nonsense. If it had not been for the Turks, not one Oriental Christian would have been alive today. The fanaticism of Latin Europe was in a fair way to destroy you when the Turkish conquest came and, with its toleration, preserved you in existence."

"Ah!" he veered round at once. "What you are saying now is very true. Formerly the Turks were not at all fanatical. And even now they are not half so bad as people think. I have heard gentlemen on board saying that there has been another revolution, and attacks on Christians in Constantinople. I, who am of the country, well acquainted with the Turkish character, find myself wondering how such false reports can be believed."

I may be wronging my unknown interlocutor, but I cannot help suspecting that, but for the firm line I had taken with him, he would himself have told me those reports were true.

"May I ask if you have friends living in Constantinople?" he inquired.

His tone had grown much less obsequious, and more respectful. I let fall Turkish names.

"But you should know Armenians also!" he protested. I replied that I should do as I thought fit. He hung about my overcoat a little, in a sort of awe; then, bowing low, wished me good night. I then resumed my interrupted exercise, musing upon his kind and all the mischief they have done to Turkey. His like beset the newspaper correspondent and the traveller with information which, if not entirely false, is so presented as to give a false impression; which information is invariably made to correspond exactly with the traveller's own taste, as ascertained by the informer. The better sort of native Christians are almost as exclusive as the Turks. This type is ever at the service of the foreign busybody. He is a product of the policy which Europe has pursued for a whole century, of interference on behalf of Ottoman Christians, and missionary efforts for their education and advancement. The result is that the Christian of the baser sort, while still technically an Ottoman subject, pays allegiance in reality to foreign Governments and asks no better than to be their hireling. Not five years ago, at the Turkish revolution, there had been a chance that these parasitical enemies would vanish, either emigrating from the country or becoming part of the Ottoman nation. To secure this end the one necessity was for the Powers of Europe to withdraw their countenance from certain internecine agitations and intrigues.

For a few weeks only did this hope appear. Then Europe made it plain that she was still the enemy of Turkey, intent now more than ever to despoil and rend her. What other construction can be put upon the fact that the revolution was considered finished, its results estimable, in the chancelleries of Europe within a year of its first outbreak, when everyone acquainted with conditions in the country knew that Turkey must remain in revolution for at least ten years? The parasites believed that their orders were unchanged. They early in the day betrayed distrust of the reformers — distrust which was, of course, reciprocated. Nay, many Europeans who had spent their lives in Turkey, and were not upon the whole unfriendly to the Turks, seeing that the revolution worked no miracle, became its enemies; forgetting that reforms need time, that to create a nation out of diverse elements is a work of education which requires at least a generation to bear any fruit; forgetting also the attacks to which progressive Turkey has been subject; not considering at all the country's or the people's good, nor yet the influence the change must have upon the Muslim world.

## Chapter I: Arrival

Of course, there is another view of recent Turkish history which sees the native Christians in the light of martyrs; the powers of Europe, chief among them Russia, as righteous judges moved by aims of large humanity. But this is altogether an anachronism. One might as well regard the Roman Catholics in England at the present day as sufferers, and justify a crusade of the Latin Powers for their deliverance. It is, besides, too violently held and preached to bear calm scrutiny. These reflections, and the ceaseless hooting of the fog-horns, kept me waking in my bunk bed. When I got up in the morning, after four hours' sleep, the hoots were still persistent. I imagined we had hardly moved from last night's anchorage. It was, therefore, with astonishment, when I went up on deck, that I saw the round towers, ruined walls, and quaint, red-roofed town of Rumeli Hisarı bathed in early morning sunlight rising from a sea of periwinkle blue. Even as I came on it the vision faded, a drift of opal fog swam in between, and by the caprice of the floating vapours the Asiatic coast appeared as a great purple shadow. Then something loomed upon our port bow, took shape rapidly, became an ironclad as busy as an ant-hill. It vanished, but another followed, exactly like it except that this was black while that was grey. There seemed no end of foreign warships in the strait. My fellow-passengers were glad of it; the Christians in Constantinople must be safe, they said; the nervous Frenchwoman thanked God with streaming eyes intent upon a first-class cruiser. And yet the scene was wonderfully peaceful as the clearing fog revealed it — the mosque of Ortaköy, with its graceful minarets, reposing on the water like a swan; the mosque and palaces of Dolmabahçe; the clustered wooden houses, brown and grey, with pretty red-tiled roofs; the wooded hills, the cypress trees, watching the sparkle of the sea on which we glided slowly. Ahead of us the soaring minarets and stumpy dome of Aya Sofia appeared in mist; then, to the right of them, and seeming high in air, clear of the fog, shone out the diadem of old Stamboul, the glorious Suleymaniyeh. This was soon hidden by an arm of Galata as we drew up to the quay, where the same pushing, yelling, seeming furious crowd of touts and porters waited as in peace-time.

I saw no difference there or on the drive up to Pera with a serviceable hotel dragoman who had released me and my luggage from the tumult, except that everything was two shades cleaner, that the horses drawing my carriage were of a more wretched description, and that wheeled traffic in the streets was less than could be reckoned normal even at that early hour. I saw tramways, but no trams, which rather pleased me. All the decent horses had been taken for the war, my guide informed me. The streets through which we passed were altogether of a Western kind, New Art prevailing in the lines of building. Except at one point where some disused Muslim cemeteries allowed a view across their cypress-tops of Stamboul and the Golden Horn, they might have been in any city from Madrid to Budapest.

The fog had lifted. It was now a sunny morning, though the air bit shrewdly as I noticed when, having been shown to an exalted bedroom at the Pera Palace, I ventured on the balcony without my overcoat. The view was dazzling. The waters of the Golden Horn ran blue below a hill of cypresses, Stamboul beyond them forming a high background; while on this side of the water there were hills and glens all over-grown with wooden houses, under red-tiled roofs, with domes and minarets and pretty graveyards. And over all the roofs and domes, above the mourning plumes of the old cemeteries, there fluttered coloured streamers decorating the whole town. These were children's kites. A very tranquil murmur rose up from the scene. My guide — himself a Christian — assured me that the city had been peaceful through the war-time, without the slighest hint or fear of riot. Why, then, were the foreign warships in the Bosphorus?

## CHAPTER II
# STAMBOUL AND PERA

The views from Pera are magnificent. There may be other charms about the place, but I have not discovered them. Suddenly, in its pretentious, modern but malodorous streets there comes a gap in the high wall of buildings and one sees the Bosphorus and coloured Scutari fringing the hills of Asia, or perhaps the Golden Horn, with Kasim Pasha in the middle foreground and Stamboul beyond. But enjoyment of such glimpses is considerably impaired by the insufferable nature of the population, which, however fashionably dressed, would seem to consist entirely of disreputable and offensive persons. These make nothing of shouldering you off the pavement, or dragging you aside with hands. No woman, I have been assured by Turkish and European ladies, however modest her appearance, is safe from insult in these streets. Stamboul is much to be preferred in this respect. There must be decent people in the place, for it is the Christian and European quarter, contains the embassies and several churches; but they have no influence upon the general atmosphere of vice and rank vulgarity. Contrasted with the stricter morals and puritanical decorum of the Turks, Pera and its neighbour, Galata, are a huge plague spot — a parasitic growth which threatens Turkey with corruption. Yet Pera and its population stand for everything which the Powers of Europe esteem worthy of protection in the Ottoman Empire. One morning, turning off the main street where it narrows suddenly, I came upon a barber's window with this legend: "Rendezvous de l'aristocratie pérote."

I stood still with amazement, staring. Specimens of the Pera aristocracy appeared within — smirking, self-satisfied, of haughty mien. "Rendezvous of the Peran aristocracy." To what a depth had a once noble word descended that it could be used to designate the scum of the Levant! I have taken Turks to see the barber's shop and shown them the inscription, to their great delight. On my first evening in Constantinople, I took a walk up the Grande Rue. On either pavement moved a fashionable throng of Greek and European demi-mondaines, with their natural complement of men in billycocks, crush hats and fezes. Every face of which I caught a glimpse in passing was animal or cunning, and seemed bent upon immediate pleasure. From brightly-lighted cafes came lively sounds of music. The picture-theatres and a place of entertainment labelled "Skating" appeared to be doing a brisk trade. I could not but remember that most of the persons who kept pushing past me, intent upon amusement, were Ottoman subjects, and that the Ottoman Empire was fighting for its life not thirty miles from this main street of Pera, where the cannon at Çatalca had been plainly heard. What recked they? They were Christians, and the Turkish Muslims. As Christians they desired the downfall of the Turks, and would have liked to see a Christian king — no matter which — arrive as conqueror. As Christians they must take their pleasure in a land of grief. The Turkish law accorded them this freedom; the Turkish police, patrolling the long street in pairs, guns slung across their backs, secured it to them. They might have been restrained or chidden for their gaiety, their theatres might have been closed until the war was over; their lives were never in the slightest danger. But they thought they were. All the rumours of intended massacres of Christians, all the reports of Turkish fanaticism which filled our newspapers at the beginning of the war, originated in their groundless fears. Invertebrate, they cringe when scared, grow insolent when conscious of another's strength supporting them. Once assured of powerful protection by the presence of the foreign warships in the Bosphorus, their demeanour became such as no other people but the Turks would have endured — so I have been assured by people who were in Constantinople all the while, and so I can believe from what I also witnessed. Bluejackets were landed for their protection last November when the Bulgarian army broke on the Çatalca lines — a crowning insult to the Muslim population, which, however, took no notice, could not be enraged. The only disorders in Constantinople during the war have been the brawls of drunken sailors from the foreign warships. At the time when the Bulgarians first reached Çatalca, and it was thought that they might take the city, a prelate of the Greek Church in Constantinople died, and was buried there with full ceremonial, Turkish troops keeping the road for the procession. Suppose a Roman Catholic army to threaten the city of Belfast — the parallel was suggested to me by an Englishman who had just come from the North of Ireland — and a Roman Catholic bishop in Belfast to die just then, would he be allowed a public funeral?

Again, on Holy Thursday of this year there was a free fight in and around the big Greek church at Pera, different groups of persons in the congregation contending for the right to carry in procession the great cross. Men were stabbed and fell; women fainted; the great cross was broken in the scrimmage; the bishop struck out with his staff upon the sea of heads.

The Turkish police upon the spot proved insufficient to put down the riot. A force of mounted men was brought from Şişli, which at length succeeded in restoring order, and conveyed the wounded to the nearest hospital.

Well, such is Pera. During my short stay there I spent the hours of daylight mostly in Stamboul. On the day of my arrival I walked into Aya Sofia and a smaller mosque nearby, of which I never knew the name. Aya Sofia had been full of refugees from Thrace and Macedonia, and though most of these had been removed to camps (so-called) upon the coast of Asia, a few family groups still remained huddled together in the great closed porch. Their appearance, the result of Christian onslaught, might well have roused fanaticism in Muslims. As I was entering the mosque itself, a Khôja asked me very courteously to be so good as to take off my hat — a thing I had not dared to do, being used to Arabs, among whom removal of the headdress is still regarded as an act of rudeness. He explained that had I worn a fez I must have kept it on. No other word or look addressed to me, on that or any other of my wanderings, suggested that the difference of faith was even recognised.

Some soldiers newly come from Asia, strolling round as I was, joined themselves to me when they found that I could read the texts and holy names upon the walls, seeming profoundly grateful for the small enlightenment. The Khôja who had asked me to take off my hat, discovering in this way that I knew some Arabic, came up presently and took me out to an adjacent mausoleum where was a fine manuscript of the Koran, the soldiers following. He made me read a page aloud in the right tone of voice, to show the custodian of the tomb that I could really do it. There were "Ma sh' Allah"s. And then they all began to talk to me in Turkish, of which I then knew only a few simple phrases. I explained in Arabic my disability with shrugs and gestures, and took my leave, amid a perfect storm of benedictions.

## Chapter II: Stamboul and Pera

Though it was still the month of February (old style) we enjoyed a spell of real spring weather, making it possible to walk with some amount of pleasure. There is a vast expanse of ruins in the middle of Stamboul, the work of the great fire two years ago. Grey mounds and bits of wall, with here an arch and there the pillar of a minaret left standing, cover a hill-side sloping to the Sea of Marmara; across which on clear days one saw the hills of Bursa and a shimmer of the snows which crown the Mysian Olympus (Uludağ). The poorer Turks, who love all open places with a view, have made of it a pleasure ground. Children's kites of many colours fluttered above it in the blue, no doubt perplexing the real kites and crows and white-winged sea birds. Groups of children were at play among the mounds, while groups of elders sat or strolled about, invariably with their faces towards the sea. But the waste was so extensive that one could be quite alone there. When the thud of cannon came out of the distance the noise the children made in playing had a certain pathos. It was the one sound of rejoicing in Stamboul. In the streets one heard no music and no singing — sounds so essential to the life of Eastern cities that I listened for them. One missed the usual jokes and laughter in the markets. Now and then the rub-dub of a drum was heard; a banner and a motley group of men and boys, white beards among them, all excited, appeared at a street-end, marching briskly to the drum's beat. They were volunteers for the front. Each morning several drums and flags set out and all day long paraded different quarters of the city. When evening came and the recruiting parties met again, the collection almost always passed two thousand, often even passed three thousand men. And all the while, along the great main arteries trained troops, newcome from Asia, were tramping towards the seat of war.

There were soldiers upon every boat which crossed from Haïdar Pasha to the Bridge, soldiers encamped at Scutari and Göztepe and many other points upon the coast of Asia, soldiers at San Stefano, soldiers in every barracks of the capital. One morning, when I took a carriage to drive out to the Edirnekapı Gate, a long file of men in khaki uniforms with grey shawls round their heads, each leading a sturdy Arab pony charged with his belongings, was passing my hotel. It stretched as far as I could see in both directions. Driving beside it down the hill and over the free bridge, I did not pass the head of the procession till I reached the open space before the Conqueror's mosque, in the heart of Stamboul. The distance must be quite three miles. And they were well appointed, well-found men, those soldiers — no longer the sad scarecrows that one used to see in Turkey. Thanks to Mahmud Shevket.

But if a stream of disciplined and well-dressed troops flowed daily out towards San Stefano, a thinner, slower stream of wretched ones set back towards the sovereign city. One evening, when returning to my hostelry along the Pera street, I noticed in the dressed-up crowd a tendency to stop and line the kerb-stone — and saw the Levantines exchanging laughs and merry winks. Craning my neck to see what the fun was, I saw:

About three hundred wounded Turkish soldiers, walking two and two, and holding hands; dragging their feet along, with drooping heads. One or two, more stalwart, kept up some kind of a song to cheer the rest. War-stained, travel-stained, their honest peasant faces each with its look of pain, they took no heed of the amusement of that fashionable throng, trudging along with their grave patience — Anatolian Turks, the most long-suffering and kind of races, to which no Power of Europe gives a thought. Therefore they are dirt to the "aristocratie pérote," who feed on them. Because they pray to God five times a day they are fanatical; because they have not been to mission schools they are barbarians; and when they come back wounded in their country's cause, their condition is fit theme for gibes and laughter. They had the presumption to fight for their own land against superior, civilised Christians who desire to take it. It is a joke to see how well they have been hacked about. The Christians line their Via Dolorosa. They are jeered at in the streets of their own capital. Ah, the fanaticism of the Turks, dear Christian brethren!

CHAPTER III
# HOUSE HUNTING

Letters of introduction are a lottery. Out of the three which I presented on arrival in Constantinople, two were productive of mere courtesy, while the third enriched me with a friend for life in Rifaàt Bey, called "English Rifaàt" from his sympathies, and to distinguish him from all the other Rifaàt Beys. No sooner was this friend informed of my arrival than he came to see me and place his interest entirely at my service. He procured for me a Turkish teacher who knew Arabic, then set his mind to gratify my strongest wish, which was to get away from Pera quickly into Turkish life. The difference of faith and customs made this desire of mine extremely hard to meet. There were Turkish hotels, he told me, but they were neither very clean nor very comfortable. All the comfort and the charm of Turkish life were in the home, and that was absolutely inaccessible. Would it not be best for me, he questioned, to stay where I was, in a luxurious hotel, where he would bring Turks to see me—anyone I wished to know—in particular a friend of his, a naval officer who knew English well, played golf and tennis, and could teach me Turkish and all other matters incidentally?

My answer was a most emphatic no. I had not come to Turkey to play golf or tennis, nor with the least desire to hear my native tongue. I had been offered introductions to some English people in Constantinople, but had refused them for fear of the conventional "good time," which means sheer waste of opportunity. I would identify myself with Turks, for the few months at my disposal, as the only way of learning what I wished to know.

He seemed astonished by this declaration, and in the discussion which ensued between us eyed me strangely. Then there was nothing for it but that I should take a house, either at Stamboul or in the country. If I did not mind the country, a house could more easily be found there. But house-rent was expensive; but furniture and servants offered problems; but the country was impossible just now, in winter—but—but— but—

I declared that were the sea hard-frozen and the land neck-deep in snow I should prefer the meanest lodging in a Muslim village to a cosmopolitan hotel in Pera.

My vehemence amusing him, he said: "Why is it that you all hate Pera so?" He had heard so many Englishmen inveigh against it. Still it was the nearest approach to European smartness to be found in Turkey; and those who sought a merry life had best remain there. Perhaps, however, I was right in my desire to leave it—again I caught him looking at me curiously—for people who knew chiefly Europeans gathered quite a wrong idea of Turkish manners. All the same he feared I should be bored to death. There would be absolutely nothing to divert me—no games, no parties, nothing. He was afraid that I should be disgusted with the people and the life. I then confessed—the thing had hung so long between us, and I felt guilty under his bewildered gaze—that I was not, I greatly feared, a proper Englishman, since the chosen pastimes of my race had no delight for me. I told him something of my

Arab life, my love of Muslims. His face then brightened with intelligence; he pressed my hand, and said that there would be no further difficulty.

What difficulty there was arose from the objection which all Turks—indeed, all Orientals—have to the intrusion of a lone man in their neighbourhood, who may—quite naturally, since he is alone—cast longing eyes upon their women. My friend declared it was a pity that I had not brought my wife with me, since her presence would have simplified the whole affair. But it would also have prevented the complete immersion in things Turkish for a term of months, which was my way of studying the country.

At last, one evening Rifaàt came to say that he believed that he had found the very thing for me. He had just that minute thought of Misket Hanum, an old friend of his. This Misket Hanum, though a European lady—real Western European (he insisted) without a taint of the Levant—had become a Turk to all intents and purposes, having from a child thrown in her lot with Muslims, and speaking Turkish as her native tongue. She inhabited a fine kiosk upon the coast of Asia. Since her father's death the house was much too large for her. He was going to persuade her to let me have part of it. Her European birth, my friend considered, would prevent her feeling shy of a male visitor; while the Turks would be quite satisfied of my respectability if guaranteed by her.

I hung my hopes at once upon this project, and when my kind friend came again upon the morrow to tell me it was all arranged I jumped for joy. He packed me off at once to see the house, writing me out a paper of directions which I was to show to anybody if I lost my bearings. Arrived at the village, I was to call first upon one Fethi Bey, who wished to know me, and Fethi Bey would take me on to Misket Hanum's. Thus charged, I took a cab down to the bridge, where without much difficulty I procured the necessary tickets at the landing-stage and presently made one of a dense crowd of pleasure-seekers—it was Friday afternoon —on the deck of a steamer gliding out into the Bosphorus. It was a brilliant day. Over the blue water the seaside towns and hills of Asia smiled a welcome, already seeming home to my imagination. Landing at Haïdar Pasha before the station of the Anatolian railway, I passed with the crowd up a broad flight of steps and through a doorway. A train was waiting. Everybody made for it, so I did likewise, shirking the natural question which presented difficulties. I could not have done better as it happened, for after half an hour of doubt and some anxiety, I heard the name that I was listening for called out by porters, and alighted in what seemed a public garden, under trees, full of a gaily coloured Eastern crowd, with a white mosque behind it, and a booking-office somewhere in its depths. Following my friend's instructions, I sought out the station-master, showed him my paper, and besought his aid. Rifaàt had decreed he was to put me in a carriage. This, however, he refused to do, protesting that the house I wanted was but two steps off. He pointed to a big kiosk across the line, and I set out to reach it. But as the road went round among the garden walls, I found it necessary to make fresh inquiries. I did so at a corner shop, a kind of cavern under trees, in which a group of men sat gossiping; again of one who led a bullock-waggon and an old man at work upon a broken wall.

"Where is the house of Fethi Bey?" was my stock question. The answer came invariably:

"Hanghi Fethi Bey?" (Which Fethi Bey?).

"The son of Hasan Pasha."

"Hanghi Hasan Pasha?" It seemed there were a hundred of that name. I could only shrug and show my paper helplessly, and none of those I asked could read a word.

The big kiosks or country houses had no names or numbers. Their gardens were surrounded by forbidding walls, their gates were high and solid, shutting out all view of them. They were distinguished locally, I found out afterwards, by natural or artistic features: "pine-tree kiosk." "The kiosk with the bright green gates." "The kiosk with the judas trees in front of it." "The kiosk before whose gate there is a big bump in the road," and so on. Add to this that the Turks have no family names, so that one is forced to ask for Mr John or Mr Richard in a land where Johns and Richards are as thick as olives! I began to realise the superhuman difficulties with which the Turkish post has to contend, and since then have had reason to admire the keen intelligence displayed on two occasions by that much-maligned department. It is unusual for Turks, unless near neighbours or extremely intimate, to call on one another in their country houses, these being regarded as essentially the home, where women can enjoy more liberty than is allowed them in the city. The men go into town for business and society. The women know the houses of their friends from childhood generally; though I did once encounter an old lady in a state of tears, who begged me for the love of Allah to direct her to a certain Pasha's house for which she had been searching for four solid hours!

Well, there I was, in a road of high blind walls with leafless trees behind them, through whose boughs the latticed upper windows of one huge kiosk peered at me mockingly. There were a hundred lordly looking gates to choose from, and not a soul who could direct me. At last I put my question to a turbaned elder in an ancient cloak, who came up slowly, leaning on a staff. I had just discovered on my paper of instructions that the house I wanted was "opposite the kiosk of English Zia Pasha" (a nickname has the value of a surname). "Opposite the kiosk of English Zia Pasha, the late Hasan Pasha's son, Fethi Bey." Thus ran the legend.

The old man understood my question, and evidently knew the house I wanted perfectly, for he was going to great lengths in explanation when, seeing my blank look, he cried out: "Turkja bilmayor" (He knows no Turkish), and hid his face in his hand. Thinking the interview concluded to my disadvantage, I thanked him kindly and was moving on, when he took sudden hold of me, exclaiming,

"Look!" I fixed my eyes upon the fingers he held up before me, while he shouted: "One, two, three, four—gate—the right side— understand?"

I did understand those simple Turkish words and set off briskly, but before I had accomplished fifty paces I was wondering whether or no to count the gate near which our colloquy had taken place. I looked round for my director. He had disappeared. And then I found I had forgotten where I started from, and how many gates I had already passed. My quest appeared so hopeless that I thought of going straight back to the station. But, before despairing, it seemed best to try one house. I therefore chose a pair of jealous gates, the nearest, and pulled the bell. It rang much louder than I had expected. The gate was opened instantly a little way. A serving man looked out.

"Is this the house of Fethi Bey?" I asked.

"Hanghi Fethi Bey?" came back the answer, slap.

I could have howled, so great was my exasperation, but at that moment someone slipped out from the garden opposite and ran across the road. My name was spoken. I saw a very gentlemanly looking youth smiling and holding out his hand to me.

"My brother-in-law expects you," he remarked in French. "We should all have met you at the station as a duty, only as we did not know your likeness, we thought that that would be the surest way to miss you. I live across the road and I was told to watch."

The bell that I had rung was after all the right one. After an hour of conversation with a group of friendly men in a Parisian drawing-room, I was taken out to see my future residence. The kiosk of Misket Hanum differed from the others in appearance only in the matter of its garden gates, which, though as high as all the others, were of open ironwork,

### Chapter III: House Hunting

allowing passers-by a glimpse of a broad gravel-sweep surrounding a high knoll on which the house stood hidden in a grove of deodars. As we drew near the door a maid came out and asked us to be good enough to walk about the garden for a minute, as her mistress had some lady visitors. Accordingly we wandered through a grove of leafless chestnut trees, a thicket of magnolias and some shrubberies behind the house, to a small lake alive with goldfish; whence we passed on through a pine coppice, a vineyard and an orchard to a sheltered rosery where Misket Hanum —a slim girlish figure— came to greet us. She was so much more youthful than I had expected that I could not repress an exclamation of concern. My companion quite appreciated my misgivings, but hoped it would not matter among Europeans. He would be miserable for life, he said, should anything prevent my coming to the neighbourhood. My whole scheme was of course improper from a Turkish point of view.

But at the first words the lady spoke all question of propriety was lost in disappointment. She remarked in perfect English that she was afraid she could not have me as she had as good as let the rooms already to a German family, old friends of her papa. She took us then into the house and—just to tantalise me, as it seemed—showed us the rooms predestined for the German family, which were delightful, looking out into the upper branches of the deodars.

"What luck?" asked Rifaàt, greeting me on my return to Pera. Hearing of my disappointment, he seemed much annoyed. Misket, he said, had let him think that she was willing to receive me; she was like his sister, and had no business to play fast and loose in this way. She had, he now remembered, murmured of a German family, but he had treated it as mere evasion, which indeed it proved. He told me not to worry, he would put things straight. In fact, when next he called, it was to tell me all was well. I was to move to Misket Hanum's, bag and baggage, on the Monday following. He more than hinted, laughing, at exertions he had undergone, long arguments diversified with little journeys to bring in diverse neighbours to persuade the lady, whose reluctance— unexpected in a European—he set down to the natural frowardness of girls.

As I now look back on them, the sixteen days which I spent at the Pera Palace were both amusing and instructive. The company consisted of a few war-correspondents and photographers, a few concession hunters, two Egyptian princes, and one Turkish gentleman, Ali Haïdar Bey, son of the great reformer, Midhat Pasha. The last named, to whom Rifaàt had presented me, took pity on my stranded state and generally spent the evening with me, in discussion of all sorts of topics. Our humours chiming, we became good friends. Unpleasant-looking Levantines, attendant on the correspondents, came and went. One horrible Armenian in particular would strut among us with a knowing air and, when questioned of the news, would say: "I have my prifate informashuns!" This man was pointed out to me, I know not why, as "the 'Times' correspondent," which he certainly was not. I worked for two hours daily with a Turkish teacher, a Roman Catholic Arab from Diyarbakır, one of the under-masters at the Galatasaray school. He proved a capable instructor, and was besides a modest and well-mannered youth, quite like a Turk in his behaviour. Though we talked together long and freely, I could not discover that he had ever so much as heard of Turkish fanaticism—Christian though he was, and mixing, as he did, continually with Muslims. Indeed, he was a most enthusiastic Ottoman, and my acquaintance with him gave me the first hint of what the revolution might be doing for the rising generation. I had to part with him, when I retired to Misket Hanum's.

## CHAPTER IV
# PINETREE KIOSK

Had I been a Balkan army, Misket Hanum could not have felt more dread of my arrival. When Rifaàt Bey adjured her to receive me as a guest she hastened to seek strength among her friends. Putting on her head-veil and "mashlak," she fled round from house to house bewailing her sad case; and everyone who came to call on her was asked for pity. To my certain knowledge she consulted a princess of the Imperial family, two pashas, two doctors, a military cadet, a dressmaker, and a washerwoman, in addition to the ladies forming her immediate circle. She was horrified to find opinions pretty evenly divided as to the propriety of the proceeding which was being urged on her. The princess argued that I could not be depraved or really dangerous, since I was recommended by a Turkish gentleman of good repute, and was a lover of Islam. Upon the whole she was advised to make a trial of me, all her Turkish friends engaging to hasten to her rescue should I prove obstreperous. The military cadet above referred to—a sterling Arab from Damascus, who when we met was first to laugh at these forebodings—advised that special watchmen should be posted round the house until they could be sure that I was not a malefactor; also that the head gardener, well-armed, should sleep indoors the first few nights to be at hand if needed. These counsels, while upon the whole they egged her on to the adventure, increased the lady's terrors, which arose from Turkish modesty; for the Muslim order of society is as prudish as a Knox or Calvin could desire, protecting a large store of hidden sweetness—a fact to which that "blessed word," polygamy, has blinded the majority of Europeans.

When the carriage which had brought me from the railway station pulled up at the gate, I was struck by the pale faces, as of creatures doomed to death, of the women who ran out to meet me. The gardener, enjoined to take my luggage—a handsome Laz from Trebizond, the same who had been chosen to frustrate my fancied wickedness by sleeping in the house the first few nights—alone had strength to smile. The women, frightened as they were, oppressed me with attentions. My likes and dislikes were their evident concern. The cook's misgivings were of a consuming nature. If there was anything that I particularly liked, let me name it, and it should be brought, if possible; though, in this war time, when supplies were far from excellent, it was hoped that I would condescend to make allowances. Fear was expressed lest I should hate the dulness of the village life—and blame them for it, seemed to be inferred. There, again, the war was responsible. There was so much sorrow—not a house but mourned some near relation.

I did my best to calm the trembling suppliants, assuring them that I was so delighted to be quit of Pera that I should not notice though I slept on stones and ate dry bread. A few words with my hostess on the subject of the Turks, revealing a wide field of sympathy, seemed slightly to relieve her mind.

"Why is it that all Europe hates us?" she exclaimed. "Why are Christians, who call themselves enlightened and well educated, so murderously fanatical against the kindest and most upright people in the world? She had lived among the Turks from childhood, with her father. "When my father died," she told me, "many European friends imagined I should leave this house and go to Pera—implored me to retire to Pera—to be safe! That shows how little Europeans living here in Turkey know about the Turks. To this day they think it dreadful that I stay on here alone with Muslim servants. But I am sure that I am safer, more respected here than anywhere in Europe."

She assured me she had never met with any wrong—nothing but kindness both from rich and poor—among these people whom the Christians were now bent upon exterminating. She had nursed the wounded in a local hospital, and wished I could have seen how good they were, and patient. Tears filled her eyes as she referred to them. She had been the only woman in that hospital, the other nurses were all Turkish gentlemen; and she had been treated with the finest courtesy. Her fellow-workers had become her friends for life. How were such lies about the Turks believed in Europe; who invented them?

She had to leave me presently, being still in much concern about the comfort of my room. I then put on a fez and went out into the garden to a shady seat. It was an afternoon of summer heat, contrasting with the wintry bareness of the chestnut grove which stretched before me, aisle on aisle. A tentative, half-wakened croak of frogs came from the little lake upon my left, hidden from view behind a mass of shrubbery. Real Eastern cries were wafted from the distant roadway. I felt entirely comfortable and in place for the first time since leaving my own Sussex farmhouse. The twigs and branches of the chestnut trees cast a tracery of shade upon the ground. I was contemplating this and smoking peacefully when the intrusion of a broader shadow caused me to look up. A very stately personage had joined me silently. His snowy turban and black flowing robe announced him as a khôja

(Muslim clergyman). With his right hand he saluted gravely, touching lips and brow. I rose and did the same. He handed me a visiting card of Rifaàt Bey's, with my name and some imagined dignities written on it in Turkish. Having read it, I saluted once again, profoundly, took his hand and led him to the seat upon my right. On sitting down we both half rose again and did the same salute, this time with smiles. To my immense relief my visitor then uttered words of Arabic—the best Koranic Arabic, pronounced with many hesitations and much search for words, precisely as a classical scholar of the Church of England would speak Latin, if obliged to do so, for the first time. I began to answer glibly in the Syrian vernacular, till I saw that it was largely unintelligible to him, when I also was obliged to use the literary language. Our conversation was thus stilted, but we understood each other perfectly.

He was, I learnt, a keen progressive, like so many quite old-fashioned Muslims. Indeed, there has always been a number of devout Muslims who regarded an unbridled despotism as of nature irreligious and disastrous to Islam. Learned doctors of religion had a large hand in drawing up Midhat Pasha's Constitution, and the theological students in the capital were its fierce supporters. It is, therefore, a mistake to speak of Islam as unprogressive save by force of circumstances. My visitor dwelt much upon the need of patriotic education, of encouragement of every local effort for self-government, as tending to relieve the Porte of the enormous burden left to it by the old tyrannical regime. The work had been mapped out, he said, and, as regarded education, well begun. Rifaàt had told him that I knew Arabic, and was a lover of Islam, and he had eagerly expected my arrival in order to enjoy a talk with me about the future of the country. He was one of the Deputies of Constantinople in Parliament, and a theological authority, I afterwards discovered. What—could I tell him— was the cause of the great outbreak of Christian fanaticism, aiming, as it seemed, at the extermination of the European

### Chapter IV: Pinetree Kiosk

Muslims, at a time when Turkey had espoused that very progress which Europeans had been preaching to her as the one thing needful? I told him my opinion: that the Christian Governments were paralysed by mutual fears, thus giving Russia's ancient hatred of the Turk the lead which resolution has in an assembly of the hesitating; that among the Western peoples the crusading spirit, now as in old days, was due to utter ignorance. He asked a lot of other questions which I answered to the best of my ability. Meanwhile, without the need of any bidding, a damsel brought out coffee and some appetising cake, of which we both partook.

While we were talking I had more than once a sense of being spied on from the house. No sooner had my visitor departed than the feeling was explained; for Misket Hanum hurried out, preceding, in order to introduce, two Turkish ladies wearing the headveil and the loose white cloak which is all that is considered necessary in the country for informal visits, and two young men, their relatives. They had come to bid me welcome to the village, and, longing, as they said, to make my acquaintance, had been watching our conversation from a window, looking daggers at the khôja, thinking he would never go. Of course they dared not "come out" —that is, show their faces to a man—while he remained. Two very pretty girls bowed to me, blushing, and held out their hands as soon as their male relatives had shaken mine. "Welcome to our country" was the burden of their greetings, which had a small point of hostility, it soon appeared, for they immediately expressed regret that owing to the wicked, cruel war, I saw it quite unlike itself, immersed in grief. But it was not to blame for that, I must remember. I was to blame for it, seemed to be implied, as representative of hateful Europe. Two pairs of great blue eyes, half-frightened, half-defiant, searched my face for evidence of anger or fanaticism. The youths, more diffident, left to the girls the task of opening conversation. Again I was asked why England hated Turkey;

again I aired my views upon the subject, this time in French, which the elder of the girls spoke almost perfectly. Misket Hanum, flurried as she was with business upon my account, soon ran back into the house, leaving us to stroll about the garden for an hour, by the end of which my visitors had lost their shyness; both boys and girls were chattering quite gaily, and I was being teased for too fanatical a Muslim. Like all the Turkish women whom I subsequently had the privilege of knowing, these girls were absolutely frank and easy, with no foolish airs, no giggles and side-glances. What we esteem the finest breeding would seem to be the heritage of the whole race, for rich and poor alike possess it. That and personal beauty are the rule, in my experience.

When the visitors had departed, Misket Hanum came out again, her hospitable labours ended, and showed me round the garden as the sun set. Her embarrassment in my society was still great; observing which, I hazarded a question that was in my mind: would she be willing to receive my wife, supposing that the latter could come out and join me in a few weeks' time? How her eyes brightened! How her tongue was loosed! I was besought to say exactly what my wife was like. Did she love the Turks as I did, or might she not object to wearing Turkish dress? Misket Hanum fell at once to planning fresh arrangements in the house and expeditions to be made when she arrived. As we passed by the shed where the gardeners, and other Lazes, friends of theirs, abode in harmony, she cried to her head man: "Madama da gelejek!" (Madame also is coming.) And when the chill of night drove us indoors, she told the news to Eudoxia, the Greek handmaid, who curtseyed and expressed grave satisfaction.

But at the evening meal we were again embarrassed. The mistress and the maid in waiting watched my face for signs of anger, as each dish appeared. The crucial test to be applied to me, it seems, was "dolmas"—leaves stuffed with rice and chopped-up meat, with yaghurt (sour milk) by way of sauce. A European, it was thought, might fling it from him. When this was set before me I cried out for joy, informing them that they had hit upon my favourite dish; whereupon both mistress and maid exclaimed in one breath: "Praise be to God."

Though I have no evidence upon the point I do not fancy that the gardener was asked to bring his pistols and his rusty scimitar and sleep outside my bedroom door that night.

## CHAPTER V
# THE NEIGHBOURS

The road which ran past Misket Hanum's garden-gate ended in one direction shortly in a flowery cliff upon the Sea of Marmara; in the other it divided a suburban township, leading out by an old mosque and village and some tangled cemeteries to open country of a mountain character. Primitive wagons drawn by buffaloes, decked with blue beads against the evil eye, the stubborn hair between their horns made bright with henna; country carts with red or yellow curtains flapping in the breeze, and now and then a well-appointed European carriage passed along it, wending to or from the railway station. The almond-trees and plum-trees were in bloom, and in the town as in the country everybody carried flowers. From Misket Hanum's garden a very English-looking path through corn-fields led down to a little harbour, consisting of a much dilapidated jetty and some wooden sheds, from which the view was of the Prince's Islands, with their summer towns set in a sea as blue as lapis lazuli. One got the same view from the wooded heights inland, with the addition of Stamboul and some more distant coasts of Europe and of Asia. My first few days, being sunny, were spent in exploration of the neighbourhood. There followed rain and mud and bitter cold, when I was glad to stay indoors and work at Turkish. The Imam of the village mosque taught me for an hour each day, excepting Fridays, and I spent much time in study by myself over the day's newspaper and a dictionary. Once or twice a week I journeyed into town to get my letters. On boat and train there was always a coterie of persons from my village who always gathered in the same coach of the train, the same position on the steamer. I soon became a recognised familiar of this group, which comprised ex-Ministers of State and high officials, officers employed at the arsenal or the Ministry of War, doctors, khôjas, and some journalists; and heard the war and general politics discussed in sad or angry tones according to the speaker's views. The Unionists (Ittihâdjilar, so called from the Committee of Union and Progress) were sad because the war, continued by their party with the hope of saving Adrianople, still went against the Turks. The Itilâfjilar (Entente Liberale party, hereinafter called the Liberals), upon the other hand, were angry at the madness, as they called it, of the Unionists in prolonging a hopeless struggle, and blamed them for overthrowing Kiamil Pasha's cabinet upon an empty boast. I soon found out that party feeling ran extremely high. There were certain people who would not speak to certain others. Men who had been talking to me in the friendliest manner would suddenly look glum and edge away when someone else drew near of my acquaintance. Most of my friends were Liberals, but two or three—and those the best I had—were Unionists. I naturally took no side in the dispute, but listened keenly to both parties with a view to forming an opinion.

One day when I had gone to town upon some errand I seemed to notice a fresh atmosphere of gloom about the streets. Meeting a friend, I asked him what had happened.

### Chapter V: The Neighbours

He said that Adrianople, it was feared, had fallen. Had I heard the cannonade upon the previous day? I had. Indeed, the noise of it so near had caused a little panic of the ladies in our village, some of whom, believing that the Christian fanatics had got through the lines, had come to Misket Hanum, as a foreign subject, to implore her to protect and hide them. Well, that cannonade, he told me, was a general attack on the Çatalca lines—really a feint to keep the Turkish army busy while a great combined assault was made on Adrianople. The Bulgarians had got the Serbs to help them, not to speak of Russian volunteers, and so the town had fallen.

He repeated: "But the news is not yet known," begging me not to mention it as yet. How came it then that everybody seemed to know it? On board the boat, as I went homeward, talk was hushed but ran on nothing else, though there was no mention of it in the evening papers. Misket Hanum had received the news before I came, and greeted me with tears in consequence.

The tidings were confirmed next morning. All the papers had it then that Shukri Pasha had blown up the citadel, with himself and what remained of the brave garrison. I believe it was a disappointment to all Turks when this account was contradicted by authority, and it was known that Shukri Pasha and the rest would go to Sofia as prisoners. They needed some great crash of heroism for their nerves; and such a crash might possibly have wakened Europe to the fact that Turkey lives still, with a passionate life unknown in Western lands.

The grief and rage felt for the loss of Adrianople by all classes of the Muslim population was intense. The other territories might conceivably become good riddance—they were mere dependencies; but this was Turkey proper—Muslim country. The loss of Macedonia and Albania did not rankle—there was no desire for vengeance in regard to that. But Adrianople was another matter. It must be regained at all costs. "Revenge for Adrianople!" was the general cry. Our house was behind none in patriotic fury. My Turkish teacher—gentle student that he was—and I both vowed to volunteer for the re-conquest of the Muslim fortress on the first occasion, meaning to march together side by side. Misket Hanum called down vengeance on the Powers of Europe. "Did they not solemnly declare at the beginning of the war that no one should gain any territory by the fighting? That was when they thought the Turks might win! Kyur olsunlar!" (May they go blind!)

All this may seem like madness to the quiet reader. In truth the Turks were maddened by a long course of injustice. The loss of Adrianople was the last straw. But the madness soon subsided, once the vow was made, and people settled down to watch events. The coolness of the army, after the first shout of rage, was, I am told, remarkable, and ominous. Our Liberal friends inclined to lay the blame for Adrianople's fall upon the Unionists who had tried but failed to save the city. But Misket Hanum would have none of it. Then it was I first discovered that she was an ardent Unionist, bearing her faith in the Young Turks intact amid continued assaults, for almost all her friends were of the other party. At that time I inclined a little towards the Liberals from having been for some days chiefly thrown with them, and spent much time—not uninstructively—in trying to impress on her the Young Turk errors.

Misket Hanum's fears of me once fairly dissipated, she became an amiable tyrant and reproved my ways. I had, of course, a cold, or a succession of colds—everybody has in Turkey in the winter— which gave excuse for feminine oppression, Turkish gentlemen and ladies were brought in by her to see me, no longer as an unknown terror, but as some wild creature she was proud of having tamed. Nothing could exceed the friendliness of these acquaintances. I was admitted fully to a little circle of advanced French-speaking Turks, of which the ladies were permitted to adopt me as a brother; while the old-fashioned men—the vast majority— assured me that their wives and daughters were much looking

## Chapter V: The Neighbours

forward to my wife's arrival. Kind messages were sent to me by women who would have perished rather than be seen of me. One most exalted lady asked me for my opinion upon a question which had long been troubling her. She had been recommended to visit Switzerland for her health. Would it be possible for her to do so, wearing Turkish dress? She had never in her life used gloves or corsets, and, being elderly, felt not at all disposed to pinch her figure or put on a silly hat. Rather than subject herself to such indignity, she would remain at home. A Levantine woman, whom she had consulted, had assured her that she would be torn in pieces did she venture to appear in Turkish dress in Western Europe. Were the Europeans really so fanatical?

I sent a message back through Misket Hanum to the effect that she could go to Switzerland in Turkish dress without the slightest fear of an insult greater than the natural curiosity of well-bred people; travelling, as she would travel, in reserved compartments, and stopping at the best hotels. I hope I did not over-estimate the West's politeness.

One morning I was walking in the garden by the lake, when a tall and very graceful woman came towards me, wearing the black charshaf, which, as worn today by Turkish ladies, is a dress of Grecian beauty. She had her veil thrown back. A white-veiled slave came on behind her at a studied distance—a second but more rustic statue. I had turned to flee, as decency enjoined, when she implored me in soft wailing tones to wait for her. I then perceived that she was weeping bitterly.

Would I forgive her, she exclaimed, wringing her hands, for coming out like this to trouble me? But Misket Hanum had assured her I was not ill-natured, had even bidden her to come to me. Her grief was very great, and I could help her if I would. Her brother-in-law, her sister's husband and the best of men, besides the greatest general Turkey had, had been reported murdered in Albania. The news was not confirmed. It was a rumour only, but it had been printed in the evening papers.

Her sister had chanced on it, and was now quite prostrate. Would I—could I—go to Pera for true? I went at once and asked the Times correspondent, Mr Philip Graves, the only Englishman I knew who was likely to have information on the subject; bringing back to those ladies hope, which proved fallacious. The news of the assassination was confirmed some six weeks later, and all that while the wretched wife was in suspense. When at length she knew the truth, her husband had been four months dead.

This is no isolated instance. In our village there were many ladies who had not heard a word of sons and husbands for six months and more; who had no notion where they were, whether in captivity, alive and well, or dead and buried; who only drank the common fount of news—an endless tale of pestilence, defeat and massacre. Their sufferings can hardly be conceived by English women, who have many interests. For a Muslim woman her husband and her children are the whole of life.

One of our neighbours who had been a childless wife for fifteen years, yet had never been supplanted in her husband's love, would not believe the news, when it arrived, that the said husband had been killed in battle at the very outset of the war; but every day expected his return or news from him. It seems probable from what I heard and saw that she will go on thus expecting him until her dying day. One of my Turkish sisters had the bitterness of hearing that her husband had been hanged, and then, soon after, that her brother had been murdered in Albania. The news in both cases proved false, but it was current for some weeks. Occasionally there were happy endings to the long suspense. I myself was witness of the reappearance of a giant officer, in perfect health, for whom his family had mourned for three whole months. The lack of surnames made it difficult for people to identify their own relations in official lists of killed and wounded, which were, besides, occasional and incomplete. After the second armistice, when news at last could be obtained from the lost provinces,

*Chapter V: The Neighbours*

in every Turkish paper one read columns of advertisements for officers and men of whom all record had been lost. "Good Muslims, of your Charity, for Allah's love!" Good Muslims are extremely like good Christians.

Then there were gruesome stories of the massacres. A lady who had fled from Monastir recounted tales of cruelty, the work of Balkan Christians, which made mere crucifixion seem a deed of kindness. Our nearest neighbour had a cousin in the madhouse, the reason of his madness being this:—

He and some other Turkish students of good family had volunteered for service in the war and, being all acquainted, kept together. One night they were on outpost duty in a lonely hut, quite unaware that the force to which they were attached was in retreat, when they found themselves surrounded by Bulgarian komitajis. The character of the assailants was so well known that all were panic-stricken, and one, who was small, managed to get into an empty barrel which was in the hut. The boy in hiding heard what followed, when the students had been overpowered. "You'll look better without that nose, bey effendi. Those lips are much too long, they hide your teeth. And now that pair of ears—those eyes—that tongue!" Such words, with the horrid crying of the victims, still more, perhaps, his own terror which prevented him from coming out and sharing the fate of those he loved, drove the youth in hiding mad, not at the moment, for he managed to lie quiet and escape, but afterwards, when he had reached a place of safety.

Mere human rags deprived of almost all that makes life sentient found their way to Turkey with the refugees. Among a crowd of wretches who were taken care of on a farm belonging to my friend Ali Haïdar Midhat, every girl and youngish woman had been violated; and children of thirteen were big with child. In our village one saw many refugees. It was nothing uncommon at the railway station to send a tray round, among persons waiting for the train, on behalf of some unhappy individual. One day, when I was called on to contribute, the object was a splendid specimen of manhood who had had his tongue cut out. I think, too, there was something wrong about his ears, but cannot be quite certain for he wore a heavy turban.

CHAPTER VI

# VIEWS OF ENGLAND

One evening when I was returning from Stamfeoul, I got on board the boat some time before it started. Choosing a seat whence I could see the mosques and the old palace looking down upon the sapphire water buoyant with little boats, I began to glance through the columns of an evening paper I had purchased on the quay. As it happened, there were sitting near me two old gentlemen, also with evening papers in their hands, who presently began discussing the report therein contained of a meeting of pro-Turks in London to protest against Great Britain's Balkan policy. I had read the notice of the meeting in my journal, so knew at once to what their talk referred. It ran like this :—

"It seems we have some friends there as in France!"

"Aye, as in France precisely—a few exalted souls like Pierre Loti, who are persecuted and derided! The English, like the French, are full of words —toleration, humanity, liberty, and so on—but when it comes to deeds those words are seen to be quite empty. The common people are exceedingly fanatical, and common people in those lands control the Government. Please God they will be punished for their perfidy. India is not contented with the course affairs are taking."

"They say that England has decided to give up India to the Russians some day."

"I don't give five paras for that opinion. England will give up nothing she has laid her hands on. The Anglo-Russ alliance is but temporary, as against the Muslims. It is a pure product of fanaticism. As soon as Persia and the Guarded Realms have been subjected altogether to a Christian yoke, England and Russia will fight furiously for the spoils."

Their conversation soon meandered off to other topics, while I watched the city growing dreamlike as the sun sank. The view of modern Europe, as old Christendom, united by a fanatic hatred of Islâm, was nothing new to me. All Muslims hold it more or less, and they are justified by the whole course of recent history. The feeling towards us English, who have not been among the active persecutors, would not have been so very bitter among Turks, who are extraordinarily philosophical, were it not for our self-righteousness: the way our diplomats, our missionaries and many private individuals in Turkey have of talking as if England were a perfect country, with no political or social evils, invariably animated in its foreign dealings by motives of humanity and abstract justice.

Many will object that to assert the contrary would be disloyal and to "give away" one's native land. Such objectors are the very persons that I have in mind, and by that very thought to "give away" admit hypocrisy. An Englishman once lectured me for three-quarters of an hour in an Egyptian train upon the superiority of England and the English in a most offensive tone, under the impression that he was talking, as he put it, to "an intelligent native." I am glad, for the good name of England, that eloquence for once was thrown away upon a fellow-countryman. Personally, having a great dislike to bombast of the sort, I am not above confessing imperfection

## Chapter VI: Views of England

even to an African. Our self-righteousness is principally to blame for the horror which has filled the East upon the recrudescence of the wicked old crusading spirit in our midst, duly reported by the Turkish and the Indian Press, at a time when Turkey was deserving of all human pity. We had talked as if fanaticism were extinct in England.

Just when the shore began to glide away, the steamer backing slowly from the landing-stage in search of room to turn amid the crowd of boats, a man I knew came up to sit by me. Seeing him salute the two old critics of the English, I begged him to present me to them. After some demur, for he declared that they were quite old-fashioned and uninteresting, he complied. Referring to their former conversation about England overheard by me, I tried to tell them what I thought the truth, that the English people who reviled Muslims did so from sheer ignorance, fostered by the Press, in which the Turkish point of view was never even stated, while long diatribes in favour of the Balkan States were published daily. I asked them to say frankly whether they themselves in these conditions would not have sided with a league of Muslim States (supposing such existed) against a Christian Power accused of persecuting Muslims, at once, without a second thought of right or wrong? To this they both assented very readily.

"But what do you mean," they asked, "by saying it was not permitted to state the case for Turkey in the newspapers? Was it by order of the Government? The Opposition would submit to no such order." There was no Opposition where foreign affairs were concerned, and in every case it was probably more apparent than real, I confessed, and tried to show the comic side of party government. (My hearers chuckled, saying that they had observed the same phenomena at home in Turkey.) As for the boasted Freedom of the Press, it had ceased to be a factor in our national life, through the fault not of the journalists themselves, but of the proprietors of journals who, desiring honours at the hand of one or other of the two great parties, were amenable to party discipline. Touching the order against publishing pro-Turkish matter, I could not say whether it emanated from the Government, or from some huge financial interest, but that such an order had been laid on the whole party Press for many weeks was a fact well known to every Turcophil in England. The friends of Turkey numbered many thousands, and were mostly to be found among the educated classes. But they had never been allowed a public hearing. As far as I was aware the only paper in all England which had published anything like a full statement of the case was The New Age —a weekly independent journal much too outspoken to be widely read.

"Ma sh' Allah!" they exclaimed, with a short laugh. "Then your country is not perfect, as they always tell us. There are faults and drawbacks in existence there as here!"

"Exactly," I replied, "and also crime and ignorance. Our leaders are not always of the first intelligence. They sometimes make mistakes, and dare not own them. Our people are tenacious of old prejudices. We are, upon the whole, a most unamiable nation, composed of quite well-meaning individuals."

When the two old gentlemen perceived that, though my tone was flippant, I was really earnest in apologising for my country's failings, they at once began to differ from me, pointing out instances of British uprightness, intelligence, pluck, amiability, and what not, evinced in past affairs of Turkey, and the more I harped on our infirmities, the more enthusiastic they became. When I parted from them in the crowd at Haïdar Pasha they were chattering together eagerly, vying with each other in pro-British ardour. "If England—the people, not the Government—will stand by Turkey we are saved. It is England's turn to Russia that has been our death-blow. There is no other country in the world where public opinion is so free and so powerful. If only the English would behold us as we are, a people struggling to be something noble

## Chapter VI: Views of England

in the world, they would befriend us though we are Muslims. They are not really such fanatics as the Serbs and Bulgars. And they would find us grateful, far more grateful than the Christians."

Those were some of the remarks to which I was obliged to listen. And they were spoken earnestly, not in the smooth and flowery language of convention which (supposing that they had not felt inclined to fight) would have hailed a loud performance on the British trumpet. In the train I came again upon the friend who, having performed the introduction, had sat listening to our conversation, helping me with words when needed. He beckoned me to come and sit beside him, and at once began:

"What you said to those two old efendis was pretty; but you know as well as I do that your Government is very clever, and does not take part against the Muslims from stupidity. Look at Sir Grey, for instance! Is he not a very clever man?"

I said that I had not the honour of his personal acquaintance, but was assured that he came of a very good family, and was considered to maintain the best traditions of the House of Commons in his speech and bearing. He chuckled and looked hard at me a minute.

"Well," he said, "you will not deny that the Liberals are the fanatics, the Conservatives the progressive and enlightened party in your country. The Liberals hate the Muslims and would welcome their extermination. We have seen it many times in my remembrance. Therefore it is a great misfortune for the Muslim world that a Liberal Government should have held the power in England at this great crisis of our fate."

I wished some Liberals at home in England could have heard him. The Liberals, I answered, might be called the English as opposed to the Imperial party (he interrupted with: "I told you they were fanatics"), that is, they gave to home affairs the first place; and, while not neglecting colonial and foreign business, would not allow it the importance which Conservatives ascribed to it. In fact they hardly viewed the

British Empire as a whole, but as England and a number of dependencies. There was something to be said for that opinion, since England still was head; and at a time when, as at present, she was on the verge of a great social revolution, the Government might be excused for being deeply occupied with home affairs. Having assigned the Foreign Office to a highly respectable man, beloved of the Opposition, thus precluding trouble in that quarter, they had hoped to hear no more of it. The Balkan war had been a great distress to them, and there was not a man among them capable of dealing bravely with the greater problems which it raised. Their so-called policy had been to drift along from day to day, trimming their sails to every wind that blew or seemed about to blow; and through it all they had been hampered by their old tradition, which had made of the Bulgarian and Armenian massacres a party cry to rouse fanaticism —a fanaticism which still lived, and which they could not now control.

"That is precisely what I told you. They are the fanatics," said my friend. "Now listen! They are doing untold harm to England, senselessly. It must be clear to everybody of intelligence that Turkey is no danger to any Power of Europe at the present time. But Russia will become ere long a general danger. Why support her in her great crusade against us, and help her to increase her power? There is another danger, which you know as well as I do. Not until the last Muslim Power has fallen under Christian rule will the Islamic world be reunited in a league of life and death, and the great revolt begin. We do not want this. We consider it would be a great disaster for the Muslims and the world at large, which should advance towards peace and universal toleration. But Europe seems to wish to force it on us. . . . I wonder how much Russia spends upon your present Ministry!"

I said that I believed our Ministers to be examples of integrity. He only shook his head and sighed:

"Who knows?" "We need the help of Englishmen," he said

after a pause, "not of the British Government, but Englishmen, in our endeavour to raise up the people. Your individuals are splendid, there is no denying, and we could trust them to deal fairly with a given charge. But the British Government is treacherous, as we have seen a hundred times. It may be, as you say, the natural consequence of a democracy; but your Government is faithless, inconsistent."

I said that there was probably no living Englishman who did not in his heart distrust the British Government, even though it represented his own party views, although to foreigners we all upheld it from a sense of patriotic duty.

"I admire that!" he exclaimed. "Would to God our people did the same thing when abroad. Instead, they grow enamoured of the country they are visiting and pour contempt upon the name of Turkey." My friend, I may remark, had never been to Europe. "When they come home again they are insufferable. They would alter everything, upon the model of the country they admire. They have no idea of the value of national character to a people struggling for existence. They confound patriotism with fanaticism, a boneless cosmopolitanism with enlightenment. The cause is in the lack of education—not mere instruction out of books—but education in the strict religious sense. You English have preserved it; you are very wise! "He paused for half a minute and then sighed: "Give us a dozen of your young administrators for a term of years!"

I asked what cause he had for thinking that Englishmen would serve the needs of Turkey better than any other Europeans. He answered that the men of other European nations when employed by Turkey remained the servants of their Governments against the Turks; whereas it seemed to be a point of honour with the individual Englishman (from what he could hear) to be true to his employer against all the world.

"But Frenchmen make as loyal mercenaries," I contended.

"Yes," he agreed, "they would not cheat us on a bargain. But the French, my friend, have this peculiarity: that every

Frenchman is a missionary of his country's language, irreligion, social chaos. The English, less attractive and less amiable (saving your presence), are the better educators. They do not make their pupils wish to become Englishmen, but by means of discipline, and the natural opposition it arouses, enable them to develop strong character."

"And the Germans?" I inquired when he had finished speaking. We had by this time alighted from the train and were walking in the twilight down the avenue of fine acacias which led past both our houses to the sea.

"We like the Germans," he replied, with a short laugh. "With a little practice and instruction they make quite good Turks. But they are too pervasive. We are much afraid of them, desiring, as we do, to keep our country."

Upon a pause he added: "Has it ever struck you that Germany and Russia have a secret understanding? Think it over!" With these words he left me, turning in at his own gate.

## CHAPTER VII
# A GARDEN PARTY

One morning I received a note from Rifaàt Bey, asking me to go and see him since he could not come to me. I found him rather seriously ill. He spoke of a desire to go to Nice immediately, as his doctor told him he required a holiday with change of air, and also counselled a slight operation, which the patient thought would be more skilfully performed in France. He asked me, was there anything that he could do for me before he went? I assured him there was nothing; he had done too much already; but in the course of our subsequent conversation I chanced to mention that the Balkan massacres of Muslims were being denied by writers in the English Press. I showed him newspaper cuttings which I had received; one from the Times, admitting that there had been murders, but not more than were customary in all warfare. The writer put the number, if I remember rightly, at 600, on the authority of some impartial European (name omitted) who had lately visited the scenes and made inquiries. I should have liked, I said, to write a stiff reply to this concoction, but lacked other authority than the published Turkish reports, which were treated in the Times and elsewhere as preposterous. It was useless to apply to the Government, which seemed to have accepted wholesale slaughter of Muslims as part of the fixed policy of Europe. I described an interview with the Minister of the Interior, in which, after hearing all I had to say, His Excellency had begged me to resign myself. The Turks had published full reports of the atrocities up to the end of December, and if the English doubted those reports, they would doubt anything. It was a "parti pris," he begged me to believe, and not to beat my heart and brains out on a wall of dull fanaticism. Any person of imagination (he as good as said) who allowed his mind to dwell on the injustice in its moral and religious bearing, must go mad. Rifaàt said he would consider of the matter and, as soon as he could get about again, would try and help me.

And here it may not be amiss to say a general word concerning massacres. It is a subject on which no one ought to speak or write who has not personal knowledge of the peoples of the Near East, sets the Oriental student's teeth on edge to hear some worthy English pietist, as ignorant as a Kurd in all such matters, raising the hue and cry against the Turks on Christian grounds. Our co-religionists in Turkey suffered under disabilities no greater than were formerly endured by Roman Catholics in England; indeed, less heavy, since they were allowed to worship in their own way and to manage the affairs of their communions freely. Privileges were secured to them. There was never anything in Turkey like the fires of Smithfield. The Muslims had so excellent a name in this respect that the Byzantine Greeks preferred the Sultan to a Latin conqueror. Before the nineteenth century, when the subject Christians, stimulated from without, began their fight for independence, massacres of peaceful Christians by Muslims were practically unknown; whereas the name of Serbs and Bulgars was a byword for atrocity in medieval Europe.

## Chapter VII: A Garden Party

Our own Crusaders deemed it holiness to massacre men, women, and children of the peoples they accounted infidels or even heretics. What made the ignorant among the Muslims adopt this custom of the medieval Christians, which the better sort detest as much as we do, and think irreligious? I believe the answer to be foreign interference of a sly and wounding nature, on behalf of native Christians, to the detriment of the Muslims— interference which has worn the look of persecution in the Muslim's eyes. How many Christians have the candour or the curiosity to take for a moment an objective view of Christendom, to stand outside its confines and admire it with the Eastern world?

Ever since the historic interview of Peter the Great with Cantimir, Voivode of Wallachia, when the latter told the Czar what profit might with patience be derived from a close study of the privileges of self-government enjoyed by Christians in the Turkish Empire, Russia has been steadily at work to ruin Turkey by tampering with Turkish Christians and arousing their fanaticism. Except in two cases—when massacres were performed by savage Kurds at the direct command of Abdul Hamid II—a Sultan whom the Turks themselves deposed with ignominy for his cruelty—every massacre has been deliberately provoked. The Eastern Christians, schooled by Russia, know the mind of Western Europe, and the use of massacres to waken sympathy; and have used them as a political weapon as ruthlessly as did Abdul Hamid. Take the instance of the Bulgarian atrocities of 1876, to which the attention of England was first called by the fervid letters of the Daily News correspondent in Constantinople. They were committed by wild bashi-bozouks when engaged in putting down a general rising planned by Russia, which rising began with a massacre of Muslims. Mr Calvert, vice-consul at Philippopolis, wrote on August 29 of that year: "The Christian Commissioners, one of whom, Yovantcho Effendi, is himself a Bulgarian, state themselves to be satisfied that deeds of great atrocity marked the commencement of the rising in May last, and that cruelties were designedly committed by the insurgents as being the means best calculated to bring on a general revolution in Bulgaria by rendering the situation of the Christians, however peaceably inclined, so intolerable under the indiscriminate retaliation which the governing race was sure to attempt as to force them in self-defence to rise."

It is the history of Muslim fanaticism. If Russia had never existed, or at least had never interfered in Turkish politics, Ottoman Muslims and Ottoman Christians might long ere this have formed a happy and progressive nation. This is why the Turcophil has always felt a little nausea when decent English people called for the destruction of the Turks upon the score of massacres; and this is why I was so anxious to obtain evidence sufficient to convince my fellow-countrymen (if that were possible in face of so robust a prejudice) that the worst of Christians were at least as bloody as the worst of Muslims.

Rifaàt was, as usual, even better than his word. On the Friday following that conversation, he came to fetch me to a friend's kiosk, where one of the most influential members of the Committee of Union and Progress was expecting us. Before a house, which looked as if it had sprung up by chance in the middle of waste land beyond the railway, in the shade of a few ragged fir-trees, a goodly company of men, some of them in fezes and the black frock-coat, others in turbans and wide-flowing robes, were sitting out on chairs in a wide circle, smoking and conversing peacefully. All rose at our approach. The host, whom I already knew, advanced to meet us, and introduced me to the lion of the day. Chairs were brought out for us; coffee followed; cigarettes were offered by a dozen hands. While Rifaàt was expounding me to the large circle, I had leisure to observe the types composing it. They were all old-fashioned Turks; only Rifaàt and my left-hand neighbour, the great man, knew any French; and they were all Unionists. My Liberal friends, who were quite French in education, spoke

## Chapter VII: A Garden Party

always of the Unionists as anti-Turkish. Here was matter for reflection!

The great man, having heard what Rifaàt had to say, turned round to me and asked what exactly it was that I required. He was a very portly individual, with one of the most sensible and kindly faces I have ever seen. I explained that an important person in the Government had promised me specific information, but had failed to send it.

"How long have you been waiting?" he inquired.

"Six weeks." At that his Excellency flushed with anger, and wished to take me off at once to see the malapert in question.

From such hot action I dissuaded him, protesting that I had no grievance, and did not see that anything but unpleasant feeling could come of a second interview with one who had already failed me. He then held consultation with some khôjas seated on his other hand, who expressed strong indignation upon my account; and, turning towards me once again, inquired if I had anything to do upon the morrow. Hearing "No," he said that one of the khôjas would call for me at eleven o'clock next morning and escort me to Stamboul, to a meeting of the Council of State. The khôja chosen for my guide rose and saluted in a friendly manner. I returned the compliment. So it was settled. Then our host proposed that we should take a walk in order to promote digestion; and I proposed that Misket Hanum's garden, which I had often been adjured to treat as mine, should be our goal.

They all seemed pleased. Wistaria, the chosen flower of Asiatic Turkey, was in riot. It tumbled over garden walls, swung down from balconies on to the road, and rolled above the roofs of humble dwellings. Its colour, in such masses, perfectly set off the wooden houses, whose tint is a delicate dove-grey, a little shiny; while its habit suited the Mongolian style of most of them. The vision of an outdoor cafe roofed with it, with great festoons down-hanging, in the form of an arcade, remains with me. We paused to look at it. The shade within, where customers sat round on stools, was green, the colour of the under-leaves, whereas the faces peering out at us were lighted with a mauve reflection from the hanging flowers. I led the way with the great man, who being, as I said before, exceeding stout, proceeded at a dignified slow pace, which was observed religiously by those behind us. He often paused to mop his forehead (for the day was hot), to give attention to some word of mine, or prod some trifling object with his cane, and his doing so would stop the whole procession, which was quite a long one and imposing, to judge from all the folks who stood to watch it. Thus it took us near an hour to pass the railway at the level crossing and descend thence by the avenue to my abode—a distance any able-bodied man could cover in ten minutes' easy walking. At last, however, we were all in Misket's garden. The mistress of the place came out in transports of delight to welcome the invasion, when once I had informed her that it was Unionist. Chairs were found and the whole party settled down to talk and smoke, and drink fresh water and relays of coffee. Newcomers from I know not where kept swelling the already mighty company; for, as I afterwards heard, the news had gone through all the village—a great stronghold of the Liberals— that the party of Union and Progress had somehow got possession of the English Bey, and was holding a great council over him in Misket Hanum's garden. At once every Unionist man ran out to join the conclave as in duty bound; while Liberals of my acquaintance gathered round us in dismay, and hiding in the shrubberies, looked daggers drawn at the intruders. Many of the company, I found, knew Arabic, whereas my Liberal friends despised that classic language and studied only European tongues. We sat talking in the garden, underneath the trees, until the chill of sunset came, when the whole concourse wandered slowly to the railway station (bowered in wistaria) to see the great man off. He was returning to Stamboul that evening. When I came back from performing this small duty of politeness I found the scene of my late garden-party held against me by a revolted group of ladies of the Liberal persuasion. Well, nice friends I had made! It was evident that I liked the gross cajolery of criminals of the lowest class! They had been watching them through the leaves devising ways of killing them. That monstrous fat old horror they had thought of drowning in the lake, only they feared that he might cause the lake to overflow and flood the garden, not to speak of poisoning the frogs and goldfish. What rapture it would be, one of these days, to go and see those bodies swinging gaily from gibbets on the Bridge. That day was near at hand, they begged to tell me.

Their tone, though mocking, had a snarl in it, which much surprised me, for those ladies were the gentlest souls imaginable, and the men of whom they showed such bitter hatred had impressed me as straightforward and benevolent. I treated the whole matter as a joke; and, when they sought to know how I had fallen into such bad company, invented several fairy tales before confessing that my aim was to get information on the Macedonian horrors, which might enable me to silence certain anti-Muslims. When that confession came at length, they all acknowledged I was justified.

"But we could get you better information," someone cried.

Much curiosity was expressed about my expedition on the morrow. Returning from it, I was plied with eager questions. But as those questions seemed to indicate a wish to ridicule men who had shown me kindness, I merely stated that I had been satisfied. In fact, I had learnt nothing that I had not known before, nothing at least to justify a fresh campaign; but I had been shown enough to prove beyond a doubt that neither the Turkish Government nor any individual Turk had invented, or even knowingly exaggerated anything in the reports of massacres which had been issued by the Committee for the Publication of the Balkan Atrocities.

## CHAPTER VIII
# A MODERN KHOJA

My Turkish teacher, one of the learned in religion, who served a village mosque and taught a village school, besides instructing a few rich men's children privately in the scriptures, visiting the sick, officiating at circumcisions, weddings, funerals—in short, fulfilling very much the functions of a parish priest, though the notion of a priesthood is abhorrent to Islam—was a staunch Unionist. I had been warned when he was recommended to me that I must not look for punctuality in his attendance, as his religious duties must of course take precedence of my requirements. On the day when he was to come to teach me for the first time, Misket Hanum, I remember, was much amused at my expecting him at a given hour. She quoted many instances of Turkish vagueness. A pupil of her own—she gave English, French, and German lessons as a favour to the children of her friends—who took his lesson usually in the middle of the morning, had once turned up at 6 a.m. and, knocking up the house, had claimed instruction as his right.

A girl, whose lesson was at three, would think it all the same to come at five, and so on. Some were as regular as Europeans, but they were the exception. My khôja was not likely to be particular about an hour. However, he arrived exactly at the time appointed, and kicking off his slippers at the doorstep, where I met him, looked at his watch and called attention to the fact with rightful pride. He was a man of thirty, of a healthy, fresh complexion. His boyish eyes had an engaging look of grave simplicity, as he stroked his trim, black beard and studied my appearance frankly. I was the first European with whom he had ever conversed, and far from finding him unpunctual or in any way perfunctory in his attendance, I must say that he came always at the hour appointed, and stayed much longer than was in our contract, which was for an hour a day. He often stayed three hours and sometimes more. Indeed, I find it true of Turks in general that, though unpunctual and lazy over casual affairs, when interested in a business they lose count of time, and so, as Europeans say, defraud themselves, since time is money.

My khôja was astonished at the comfort of the house, which was quite plain as judged by English standards, and fell in raptures with the garden, which he frequently compared to Paradise. The song of the nightingales suggested to him verses of the poets; as also did the wind in the trees, the shade, the sight of flowers or ripening fruit, the hum of bees or other natural phenomena, for which he never ceased to praise the great Creator of the world.

At first he brought me for our studies an old-fashioned primer, which began with the alphabet and ended with an exposition of the Muslim calendar, together with some moral and religious stories. This we read together while he indicated with a pointer every word. He was apologetic from the first about this book for me, admitting there were better works upon the market. When next he went to town, he said, he would procure some of them, as he had long desired to do, for

## Chapter VIII: A Modern Khoja

the requirement of his little school. I had already several of my own procuring—indeed, I had started a collection of modern Turkish schoolbooks under the guidance of my Pera teacher, who had been anxious that I should examine the new course of education—but these, he said, were too advanced for us to start on. There was a proper ladder to be climbed, up which no step must be omitted by an adult any more than by a child. He had his system. And in the intervals of work we capped Koranic texts or talked of the day's news.

At last, one morning he brought me a small parcel of schoolbooks, one of which, entitled "Altun Kitab" (the Golden Book), he said was splendid. We at once began to work at it; but, as I read, I must confess that I was filled with pious horror. It began harmlessly enough with praises of school and diligence in study, reverence to parents, love of friends and brethren. But when, proceeding, I read statements like the following, I could only gasp and ask my teacher what it meant—

"TIME IS MONEY."

"To waste no minute of our time but always work means money." "Whoever recognises time as money, always has his pockets full of money."

"THE WAY TO GROW RICH."

"Hoseyn had resolved to become rich. Hoseyn did not, as greedy children do, spend all the money which his parents gave him at the sweetshop or at the fruit-seller's. He liked to save money. He was always saying: If I can only save a mejidi, I shall cause it to increase, I shall have found the way to become rich. . . . Husain had resolved to work at a trade and in that way to become rich. Lo, Husain's money-box was filled with ten-piaster pieces. When it came to opening it he found much money."

"With this money he purchased a small basket. This basket he filled inside with matches, paper, pens, and such like trifles. He went to the bazaar. By degrees he became a good seller. A few years afterwards he took a shop with plate-glass windows, which he stocked with finer merchandise. By such means he became the owner of a great emporium. Today the largest store in all the markets is his property. He is rich and at his ease. Lo! Great riches thus arise from little savings. One has only to save money and then use it in a trade."

"They say that gold is a yellow snake which bites the body. A pretty saying! But in the struggle of life we need it as a weapon. With that we can overcome every adversary, even fortune, and gain such a victory that time will applaud us, saying 'Well done!'"

"To grind the wheat to flour, of which we make our bread, mills are necessary. Mills are of three kinds. One turns by wind, another by water, and the third by steam. The wind and water mills work slowly. The steam mills quickly make quantities of flour, and naturally for this reason gain much money. If in the future you should desire to do a service, work to become the master of a big steam mill. By this means very many have grown rich."

There was much more to the same purpose. In short, the whole book seemed, as far as we had gone, to be a work of Mammon, pernicious, against true religion. I protested to my khôja that it put this transitory world above the other, and made no mention of the power of God. With dignity he bade me wait until we reached the end; and, in fact, towards the end there were some passages of a religious tendency. The last thing in the book was this small parable entitled:

## "KISMET."

"Do not listen to such empty sayings as 'Well, that was not my fate' (Kismet). 'What was in his fate came out in his spoon.' Everybody's fate is one and always present. God gives the fate of each into his own charge. Weli, one day when on his way to school, met a grape-seller. The bunches hanging from the edge of the basket were extremely fine. Weli longed for the

## Chapter VIII: A Modern Khoja

fine grapes. He wished to buy twenty paras worth. The seller of the grapes was an aged fruiterer. After weighing the grapes on the scales he gave them into Weli's hand. Weli took the grapes, but, slipping somehow from his hand, they fell into the mud. The old grape-seller, seeing the grapes thus fallen in the mud, was very grieved. Poor Weli tried to find some consolation by saying to the grape-seller: 'Well, it was not my fate.'

"The grape-seller replied: 'It was your fate, but you did not know how to take it!' Weli pondered much upon that word. From the grape-seller's remark he understood that everything in the world is man's fate. Only every opportunity must be taken. And he must know how to work."

"Well," said my teacher, "now do you understand the purpose of this book?"

I did not altogether, I confessed; for in spite of the sound sense of this last parable and a little piety-infused towards the end, the little work appeared to me to preach the faith of Mammon, God of Europe, which I hate like a good Muslim. My khôja then informed me I was too fanatical. He invited me to put apart all prejudice and then consider whether, while Christendom had gone too far in worldliness, Islâm might not have gone too far in carelessness of mundane things. God, the Almighty Maker of the World, he said, did not intend good men to leave the world aside, resigning its affairs to rascals and to unbelievers. This could be proved from Scripture wherein rules were laid down for the conduct of the faithful in the marketplace, the seat of power, the battlefield, and so on. Yet that was what had happened in the Guarded Kingdoms and elsewhere.

Religious people were unpractical and loved retirement. They spoke of money as a cause of sin, and in their hearts despised the rich and powerful. They were loth to meddle in affairs, with the result that there was nothing left to check the ambition and the avarice of evildoers. All this was named as the result—though it might with equal justice have been called the cause—of their subjection to unbridled despotism. Such a despotism was against the teaching of Islâm which stood for mutual responsibility of governor and governed, for equal opportunity and active citizenship. Was it not natural that reformers faced with such inertia should try in the public schools to rouse the scholars to personal endeavour? The chief need of the Muslim population was prosperity, which could only be attained by means of private wealth. And, as the hope of gain or high preferment had always, in all nations, been the chief incentive to exertion, was it not reasonable that, in these instructions, money should be given the importance which it actually has? A measure of ambition or desire of gain may be desirable if associated with love of country, mercy, justice, and consideration for the needy—all which virtues were (if I had deigned to notice) taught as essential in this Golden Book. I was further bidden to remember that the work in question was not designed exclusively for use in Muslim schools. It might be read in schools where Muslims, Jews, and Christians—Islam, and its two branches—studied side by side. It would, therefore, be unfair, these children being at the teacher's mercy, to give instruction there too strong a Muslim tone. The rich men of the present generation, he asserted, were useless to the country as a rule. They had gained their wealth by plundering the country, and now clung to it, regardless of the country's need. How much had been given by the rich for national defence, and how much by the poor? He could inform me. Very rich men indeed had subscribed exactly one pound Turkish, while porters in the streets gave all their savings. The present rich, or most of them, had battened on the land in Hamidian days; and now their only thought was to preserve their gains, sooner than part with which, they would, he verily believed, at any time betray the country to the Czar of Russia. It was necessary to create new wealth, new culture, new intelligence out of the common people—all of them, please God—by education. My teacher concluded this long exposition with a prayer to God that all the peoples and religions of the Empire might presently be brought together in one nation and dwell together on an equal footing in mutual respect and love.

This conversation took place in the garden when our lesson was concluded for the day, and as I escorted my professor afterwards upon his homeward road. After leaving him, while I retraced my steps through cornfields sloping to the sea, with summer palaces in gardens here and there among them, I felt hopeful for the future of the Turkish Empire, if Europe would but give the land a few years' peace. But there were other and internal difficulties in the way of that triumphant course of general progress for which my Muslim khôja worked and prayed. Of these I had a pretty sharp reminder immediately on my return to Misket Hanum's garden.

## CHAPTER IX
# OTTOMAN GREEKS

In Misket Hanum's garden I found visitors. Three bareheaded, bare-faced, black-haired, comely maidens were with my hostess on a seat beneath the deodars. Misket had talked to me about them previously. They were Greeks from a village up the Bosphorus—fearless, self-respecting girls who earned a modest living by their work as dressmakers, journeying from house to house. At one time they had gone to Christian houses only; but latterly, by Misket Hanum's recommendation, had worked for Turks as well. As they themselves informed me they were petted by the Turkish ladies, and treated by the men with all respect. Yet they dared not let their parents know that they had ever been employed in Muslim houses. Had the fact been but suspected in their village they would have been ostracised, perhaps stoned; for ignorant Christians are as fanatical as ignorant Muslims. A native Christian girl who marries a Muslim is killed as a sacred duty by her nearest relatives if they can get at her. On the steamer on which my wife and I travelled to Marseilles at the end of July, there was such a girl among the steerage passengers. Her brothers had beguiled her into accompanying them to America where her Muslim husband was already trying to make money. At Marseilles they performed her murder in a curiously open manner, seeming to think the deed would be applauded in a Christian country.

These Greek dressmakers, therefore, gave it out, at seasons when they were employed in Turkish houses, that they were working for a European, Misket Hanum, who thus acquired a reputation for extravagance and love of finery. They gave her house as their address in case of letters, and generally came to stay there in the intervals of work; Misket Hanum, like the Turkish ladies, keeping open house for women. Yet, though they owned to being much indebted to the Turks for kindness, they hated them, as I discovered presently; and did not see how any Muslim could really be regarded by a Christian as a fellow-creature. Seeing me in a fez, they took me for a Turk at first, and were going to withdraw when Misket Hanum introduced me, with a touch of malice, as an Englishman who much preferred the Turks to "Greeks, etcetera." At that they all broke out:

It was impossible! A European could not really like the Turks! What was there in them to inspire a liking? They were good-natured, truly; so were many animals. But were they not barbarians, and cruelly fanatical? Did they not keep their women in seclusion? In a word, they were not Christians. How could anyone prefer them? As a return for Misket Hanum's little thrust, all three declared their firm belief that if I wore that hateful head-dress and pretended to love Turks, it was simply from terror of my hostess, who might otherwise have turned me out of doors.

"Why, what have you against the Turks?" cried Misket Hanum. "Is it not true that when your father's house was burnt one night, the Turks, and not your precious Christian brethren, took you in, and got up a subscription for you?"

That was true, the girls admitted; the Muslims often did kind actions, which, however, could not blind a Christian to their utter and essential wickedness, the product of a false religion. It was known that they esteemed it holiness to kill a Christian when they got the chance. As for this poor, wandering Englishman, how should he know anything about them, having just arrived! It was evident that he took his cue from present company, for peace.

At this point I was moved to say that I knew something of Muslims, having spent a great part of my life with them. I asked these girls to give a single instance of Muslim fanaticism, not hearsay, but their own experience. The two elder appeared disconcerted by the point-blank question; but the youngest, nothing daunted, answered hotly:—

"I have heard them call out 'giaour' (infidel) behind me in the public street." The horror of this accusation hardly reached me. It resembled that made by the Christians of San Stefano to M. Lausanne when he was inquiring of the conduct of raw Turkish troops from Asia who had encamped there by the thousand during many weeks: "Shocking! One of them kissed a girl the other day." I had to struggle with a strong desire to laugh before replying: "That is nothing. I have been stoned by Muslims more than once."

Their astonishment at that remark was very great.

"And yet you like them? It is hardly possible. You are joking, certainly. Why should they have stoned you? And, if they stoned you seriously, how did you escape?"

I assured them I was very far from joking. The thing had happened to me once in Hebron, once in a village northward from Jerusalem, and three or four times in the Muslim quarter of Beirut, which eighteen years ago was very rough indeed. My only crime had been to wear an ugly English hat.

"So that is why you wear a fez at present, is it?" sneered the eldest of the girls; nevertheless she begged me to proceed with my narration and say how I escaped from those fanatics.

Not being a native Christian, I informed her, and therefore not having fanaticism on the brain, I on each occasion had looked upon the stoning merely as a piece of impudence involving danger to my horse and me. I simply rode my horse at the assailants, desiring to know what they meant by throwing stones at us, and invariably I was supported by the sense of justice of the crowd. Once in the outskirts of Beirut, a friend who was with me had just thrashed the ringleader—a boy about fifteen—within an inch of his life, when the father of that boy, with other elders, came upon the scene. The men were fully armed. We looked for trouble. But no sooner had I told our tale to the newcomers than the father pounced upon his son and administered a second hiding, still more awful than the first. When they discerned the moral of my tale, the three girls bridled highly and disdained it, observing that the case of Europeans was entirely different. The eldest dropped a brief conclusive word to the effect that Muslims were not Christians so could not be tolerated. She then turned to Misket Hanum and in the same chill tone congratulated her on having found a guest after her own heart.

I had many subsequent opportunities of studying the point of view of ordinary Greeks, for these girls were often in the house and our cook was also Greek and fond of argument. I never ceased to marvel at its pure fanaticism. They really liked the Turks of their acquaintance; that is to say, their own experience would have made them tolerant, but for the instruction which they had received from priest and parents, in which they hurriedly took refuge if accused of such a liking. They were gentle girls, incapable of harming anyone; yet I have heard them earnestly maintain that the great persecution of Muslims at that time going on in Macedonia was justified upon religious grounds; though they changed their tune directly it was known that the Greeks had suffered too. Some

*Chapter IX: Ottoman Greeks*

Turkish men, who visited our house habitually, took delight in teasing them until they showed fanaticism. Then they would turn to me and say:

"Amazing, is it not? In this century! But all Greeks, without exception, are like that."

The Greeks of Turkey were not always like that. Of old, when their women veiled like the Turkish women, when their men wore fez and turban like the Turkish men, there was no such bitterness between the two religions. If they are "like that" today it is the outcome of a century and more of anti-Turkish propaganda, first Russian, then Hellenic. How many Turkish subjects have thus cunningly and patiently been trained to be a barrier to Turkish progress, to prevent the realisation of my Muslim khôja's dream of peace and goodwill!

There is an aspect of this Christian question which has not been touched upon by any writer that I know of. It is the utter helplessness of the Christian subjects of the Porte before the Muslims, as compared with their immense pretensions. Their pride is not in what they have achieved themselves, but in what their co-religionists have done for them. They have seen province after province taken by the Powers from Turkey, and made into an independent Christian State, and they glory in each loss to Turkey as their victory; forgetting that, but for the interference of the Powers, Turkey would have lost no territory in Europe, or if she lost it for a moment, would have soon regained it. All the achievements of the Western world, in every field, they claim as theirs upon the score of Christianity. They have assimilated themselves in dress and manners to the Europeans, who have established privileges in the Ottoman dominions, and incline to claim those privileges on the strength of mere resemblance. When one remembers that these people are the conquered race, and that they constantly announce themselves as future conquerors, with talk of turning Aya Sofia into a church again, and crowning a new Constantine before its altar, it is a wonder that the hatred should appear on one side only. Yet so it is. The Turks dislike the Greeks—chiefly, I believe, on grounds of roguery—but laugh at them; they do not hate them.

"Oh," said the friend, who, for his quiet judgments, I had chosen for my mentor, when we broached this subject; "the hatred that they have for us is imposed on them, a kind of dogma. They hate the Armenians, Bulgars, Catholics with another, much more lively kind of hatred, I assure you. If Europe would but say decidedly that Greece shall never have Constantinople, that no more territory shall be taken from us, those people might become good subjects, like the bulk of the Armenians, who see now that they cannot hope for independence, and prefer us to the Russians."

Among the cultured, cosmopolitan Greeks of Constantinople one occasionally finds a cordial liking for the Turks. A Greek of this sort who was interested in my studies invited us to his island villa towards the end of my stay in Turkey. One evening, as we smoked together, looking out upon the sea and the many distant lights which marked the entrance to the Bosphorus, he let fall this strange saying: "You cannot say much for the Turks that would appeal to English people, for they are unbusinesslike—a fault for which commercial Europe will never forgive them. But you can say with truth that they are generally good and kindly while the Christians of this country are—well, 'wicked'; I can find no other word for it."

I cannot honestly endorse that judgment, in so far as it concerns the poorer peasant Christians, whom I know and like. It may be true of the rich Levantines; I cannot say. But the poorer Christians are not wicked; only they have been misled, and schooled to great intolerance, at a time when Muslim education tends the other way. After I had been two months in Misket Hanum's house the Greek cook asked me: "Do you truly like the Muslims? Surely it is only a pretence. We have watched you and feel sure you are a Christian. Why, then, do you like them?"

She seemed really worried. I gave some reason which occurred to me. She thought it good, and quite agreed with me—on natural ground.

"But still they are not Christians," she suspired.

"It is so puzzling." It was the supernatural aspect of the case, at war with facts, which worried her.

## CHAPTER X
# THE WOMAN QUESTION

The nightingales were singing night and day; the croaking of the frogs waxed deafening in the evenings; hosts of tortoises which had been hibernating in the thickets came out and basked upon the kitchen-garden. I fell into a very lazy way of life, the garden being large enough for exercise, and far more pleasant that the dusty roads. It also was a place of concourse and society, where all our friends foregathered in the afternoons, and strangers might be met at any time. Misket Hanum told me that her father had encouraged people to resort to it, until the place became regarded almost as a public park; and she herself had no objection to their coming so long as they refrained from damaging the trees and plants. The visitors were chiefly women, whose appearance added beauty to the vistas, their white-draped figures looking statuesque against the mass of leaves, and ghostlike in the shadow of green aisles. But their presence made my walks uneasy, for I fled before them; though it sometimes happened that in act to flee I was recalled by merry laughter; they were ladies I knew well. I was often told that my ideas were too old-fashioned, and asked to recognise the great advance the Turks had made upon the ways of my beloved Arabs. Yet the voices of the women died as we drew near the public road, and in their outdoor talk with me I could detect the flavour of an escapade. Lest anyone should think that my veiled friends were, all of them, the wives of some old Bluebeard, or had ever been immured in "harems," let me say at once that such a notion is quite antiquated. Polygamy is still established as a principle, but little practised among the Turks of today. In cases where a married couple have no children a second wife is generally taken with the consent, or at the instance, of the first. The pride and independence of the Turkish ladies is accountable for much of the polygamy to be observed in recent years. Life at Constantinople being charming, they refuse to travel. Consequently, when a husband went as governor to Baghdad or Damascus for five years at least, he took with him, as consort, a Circassian slave, who, possibly, would urge him on to further matrimony, feeling lonely in a foreign land. Apart from this, plurality of wives has ceased to be the custom, save for Sultans. On the other hand divorce is very easy, so that men and women with a taste for change may gratify it. I know a lady who has had seven husbands and speaks of her various children as "that hateful Ahmed's girl," "poor Hilmi's boy," and so on.

Instead of being restricted to her husband and her brothers, a modern Turkish lady's male acquaintance is extended so as to include her cousins, and all kinds of relatives by marriage, making a large circle. For these she goes unveiled, and dresses charmingly; for other men she is a shrouded phantom, quite unrecognisable, belonging to a separate world, the world of women. It is but natural that adventurous, bright-witted girls, who have been brought up in the European way of thinking, should be constantly seeking to enlarge their circles, urging their relatives and bosom friends to marry some outsider, that they may have another man to whom they may "come out" from veils. Misket Hanum, who had sworn to wed a Turk, was constantly adjured to do so quickly for the pleasure of her friends. By a kind of legal fiction, since only a near relative could lodge with a lone woman in a Turkish house, I was made a relative of Misket, and so, upon the score of an imagined sisterhood, accessible to all her circle. Such quibbles are by no means rare where it is a question of enlarging women's spheres. These will probably go on extending till they are as wide as those of Englishwomen, including all the eligible and polite, when the veil will be no longer any hardship, but a mere withdrawal from the crowd.

In the country one occasionally saw a man accompanying the women of his house in walks abroad; the man invariably strolled before, the women following; but it was thought a strange proceeding even there, while in the city it was quite unheard of. Outside the privacy of house and garden the men and women of a family go different ways. It is improper for them to be seen together. This being so, the Turkish ladies have a grievance in the latitude their men claim with regard to Europeans. A Turkish man will travel with a French or German woman in the train, sit next to her on the steamer, walk about with her in town, not knowing that the black-shrouded, white-gloved figure passing and repassing is his jealous wife. And when charged with misbehaviour by the latter he will justify his conduct by the European standard and blame his wife for lack of knowledge of the world. How should she know the world? She knows her own restrictions. The women have, however, one advantage in being quite unrecognisable when in outdoor garb.

A lady, coming from Stamboul one evening to our garden, where she had arranged to meet her lord and master, told us: "I passed my husband on the bridge this afternoon when I was walking with some friends, and gave him a good nudge in passing. He stood still, turned and stared, seeming much interested. I had given him a feeling of adventure. You will see!"

She shortly charged her husband in my presence with having felt a moment's tender interest in a veiled one who had nudged him on the bridge. The wretch retorted that he had, in fact, stood still a moment looking after her, debating whether he should give her into custody.

Misket Hanum, who, as Turk and European, enjoyed the freedom of both worlds, assured me she preferred the Turkish ways, and loved the real old-fashioned Turks more than the moderns. Yet she could be the European on occasion. I remember, one fine Friday afternoon, she had arranged to travel into town with me. As it happened there had come a visitor to lunch—the same young Arab from the military school, who had felt such strong misgivings at my first arrival. Much to my astonishment, Misket begged and then commanded him to come with us. He, being too polite to say "No" flatly, hemmed and hawed; but when our hostess left us for a moment, he flung himself on me, imploring me to help him—I, who understood! Misket was the only woman he had ever spoken to outside his family. He loved and venerated her extremely, but as for going out with her—why, he had never even gone out with his mother since he was a baby! He would die of shame; and would, besides, pretty certainly be placed under arrest if the commandant of the school should get to hear of the proceeding. He was shocked at her proposing such a thing. Misket Hanum had not before encountered so correct a Muslim, for she was amazed at a refusal which to me seemed natural. Most Turks are now accustomed to the Western view of women, and have two standards and two manners which they use at will.

If the men assert their right to mix with European ladies in the European manner, the women not unnaturally claim an equal licence in regard to European men of decent standing when brought near to them. The free intercourse which I enjoyed with a whole coterie would not have been allowed to any native of the country. Well do I remember a good Muslim youth who came to call on me, complaining of the conduct of an older lady who had been sitting with us in the garden when he came in sight, but then at once withdrew.

He cried: "What nonsense it all is! She talks unveiled to you, a stranger, and hides from me whom she has known a baby!"

There is a good deal of nonsense in it all in these days, and there is unfairness in the preference of Europeans. The argument that we are used to seeing women constantly, while Turks are not, holds good up to a certain point. The risk of sudden passion is much less with us. But should the flame break out—as may well happen, for the Turkish ladies are exceedingly attractive—the disaster, on the other hand, is greater. For a Muslim woman is not under any circumstances allowed to marry a Christian man; the old pride of Islâm forbids it; though the reverse, the marriage of a Christian woman by a Muslim, having a taste of conquest, is permissible. If a Turkish girl does wed a Christian she must flee the country, leave her family for ever, and give up her property. Even supposing that she does this gladly, her chance of happiness is small, for Turkish women, however much they hanker after European manners when at home, are soon disgusted with them in experience, and have been known to die of homesickness. The educated Turk today has no objection to the abstract notion of allowing Muslim maidens to wed Europeans in the time to come. But for the present it is quite out of the question, public opinion being fierce against it. While this is so, the growing fashion among Turks of taking wives from Europe should, I think, be strongly deprecated. We are not yet upon an equal footing; and until we are, such intermarriage— commonly with women of no character— will be injurious. There have been brought into honourable Turkish homes women whom the husbands' mother, sisters, cousins well know to be undesirable, though obliged by custom to receive the bride with open arms. Polygamy being virtually extinct, and women somewhat in excess of men, it follows that, if Turkish men of good society seek wives in Europe while their women are restricted in their choice to Turks, a number of well educated ladies must remain unmarried. Already one perceives the nucleus of a feminist movement, which in another generation will, no doubt, be formidable.

This concern of intermarriage has become a problem in the last few decades, and is bound to gain importance in the course of time. Islam has been called an enemy to civilisation too curtly, as I think; the fact being simply that she has not yet arrived at a modus vivendi with modern life. The process of experiment in that direction is at present going on in Turkey, among the one "white" race the Muslim world possesses. Its consequences to humanity at large are of such moment that one is amazed to see the process hindered and opposed by Europe. One of the great complaints of Ottoman Christians is that, while the Turks may see their women freely, the Turkish women are kept jealously secluded from them. Their grievance is not quite so reasonable as it seems. Formerly the native Christian women used to veil and keep apart in exactly the same manner as the Turks. While that was so there was, of course, no grievance. If from a wish to ape the Europeans, their protectors, the native Christians let their women take a liberty in dress and bearing which to the majority of their compatriots, and even to some Europeans, seems indecent, they have themselves, and not the Turks, to blame for any inconvenience which may thence accrue to them.

The coterie to which I was admitted upon terms of intimacy was, as that fact proclaims, rather more French than Turkish, though no member of it had, I fancy, been to France. The ladies read French books and periodicals, and were but a few days behind in their discussion of the newest play, the latest novel, the last sensation in the way of crime or scandal rousing Paris; while the gentlemen were equally well informed upon political events in that far country. Things Oriental they

## Chapter X: The Woman Question

looked down on with indulgent, sentimental pity as old-fashioned and a trifle barbarous.

A chief cause of this alienation of a section of the upper classes from the Turkish people has been the lack of Turkish education of a modern kind. Only one good modern school— for boys, of course— existed until lately; while European mission schools were plenty, and offered obvious advantages when the first object of the scholar was to gain the practice of a foreign tongue. The sons of high officials of the old régime either attended such schools, or had foreign tutors in the home. The girls had European governesses—often of a disreputable class, for the parents were not skilled to choose—quartered upon them. "Had" I have written, but I might have written "have," for some of the specimens I met this time in Turkey were quite unworthy of a post of trust.

My wife was asked by a girl of eighteen to recommend her a good English governess. Her father, a widower, desired to find one, but had no means of telling good from bad. They dressed alike.

"I had one once," she said, "a Mrs Johnson. But she was bad."

"What did she do?"

"Nothing at all. That was just it. She lay in bed all day and drank wine. And father did not know how to get rid of her. He could not, of course, be rude to a European lady, who was in our house, alone, without a friend. He gave her, I believe, no end of money, just to go."

Oh! Those governesses! The havoc they have wrought in decent Turkish homes! The best of them have done much mischief by their inability to see that innocence can perfectly consist with candour upon topics which Europeans cover with a sentimental veil; the worst have dealt in actual corruption. When someone asked a Turk of my acquaintance if he was not going to provide a governess for his children, he answered: "Do you think me then so bad a Muslim that I should give my son for guide a secret agent of our foes?"

"Only think! "Misket once said to me. "One of the girls who comes to me for lessons—a girl of twelve—knows every river and mountain, every department and chef-lieu in France, all the dates of the Merovingian kings, and yet cannot tell the date of Abdul Hamid II, nor the names of the Anatolian vilayets. With me she is beginning Turkish history—she said that she had never heard of such a subject of instruction—and geography and manners."

In truth, the need of national and patriotic education—more especially for women—is a crying one; the Turks have been so cheated and misled on all hands by their foreign teachers. There was another subject on which Misket Hanum, as already stated, differed strongly from the greater number of her neighbours; that of politics. She was an ardent Unionist, while they were Liberals; and it was to me a marvel, seeing the fierceness and the frequency of their disputes, that our circle held together for a single day. Our friends, being good enough to wish to win me to their side, kept dinning in my ears the evil doings of the Unionists.

"But they are the progressive party, are they not?" I asked, considerably puzzled, for in England I had heard the Young Turks blamed for rash attempts to force things European wholesale on an Eastern race. "They aim at modern progress. How is it then that you, who are so far advanced in that direction, object to them so strongly?"

"Progressive!" came the shriek. "Well, hear and judge! Woman's emancipation is a part of progress, is it not? When liberty was proclaimed, some women of the educated sort, as capable of good behaviour as the men, supposed that they might go about more freely. They were arrested, fined, imprisoned. One poor girl was sentenced to three years' imprisonment for throwing back her veil and drinking off a glass of arak in a public place. It was a piece of bravado, of vulgarity, if you like; but was it worthy of so great a punishment? And do they ever blame those others who assail us modern

## Chapter X: The Woman Question

women, spit at us and curse us if we wear a thinner veil or a more fashionable skirt than usual? Before the Constitution we felt no such tyranny. They, progressive! Why, they are most pure reactionaries!"

"I don't care what you say," cried Misket Hanum, "the Unionists are right and you are wrong. As for their severity towards some ladies, those ladies brought it on themselves. Did not they, when admitted to the theatre, tear down the wooden bars which set apart their gallery, and misbehave themselves each time they were allowed some liberty?"

"It is all their fault," she would explain to me. "They do not know how to behave; they are as yet unfit for greater liberty." In proof of this assertion she told stories illustrative of the tragic ferment among women since the revolution.

When the great ball in honour of the Constitution was given at Fener Baghcheh, a friend of hers informed his wife that he was going. His wife forbade it. He said that he was grieved to have to disoblige her, but, as a steward of the dance, was bound to go. There was a furious scene; the wife declared it was a sin for him to jump about with brazen-faced, half-naked women; but all the same, the husband went. The wife went, too, but secretly. She prowled about outside the lighted building till she found a waiter to whom she gave her husband's name and a brief message, to the effect that someone wished to speak to him upon important business. The husband fell into the trap, when she chastised him soundly with a weapon, she had hidden underneath her charshaf. He, in a rage, divorced her then and there, in presence of the crowd which quickly gathered. But she did not care. She had, she said, done justice on an evil-doer.

Again, one day when Misket Hanum was going to Stamboul a fight broke out between two ladies in the women's cabin on the boat. She helped to separate the combatants, who turned out to be friends of hers. She heard their story. They were advanced young ladies, who had been close friends from childhood. They had always vowed that, when they married, each should "come out" freely to the other's husband. They did marry, and the men approved their vow. One day the husband of the one happened to be visiting the other married couple in their Yâli (seaside house), upon the Bosphorus. His hostess, from desire to do him honour, put a highly scented towel in his bedroom. When he got home his wife first sniffed the air, then flew at him. He came to her reeking of the chosen perfume of her bosom friend. And when she met that friend in the harim compartment of a steamer, her first thought was to tear her piecemeal.

A far more dreadful thing had happened very lately. A Turkish girl, consumptive, had been sent off to a sanatorium in Switzerland. News came to her relations in Constantinople that she was worse and could not live much longer. Her sister and the sister's husband, both of them members of the "advanced" set of Turks, hastened to her bedside. The sister held long consultations with the doctor, which, no doubt, looked bad, as she did not know how to behave with Europeans, for which her husband shot her and then shot himself in presence of the dying girl, who, maddened by the sight, sprang out of bed and stamped upon the dead man's face. In spite of anecdote and representation to the contrary, however, I still considered Turkish women hardly treated by the Unionists, judging by the few of my own circle, who were highly civilised.

On my next visit to Stamboul I broached the subject, over luncheon, to the man who, since the departure of Rifaât Bey, was my most confidential friend in Turkey; at the same time asking him to tell me which of the two parties was in truth progressive, which reactionary. His reply was: "You must find out for yourself."

For himself, he was a Unionist, he said, though there were persons in that party whom he heartily disliked. But he would not give me his ideas, nor seek to influence me in the least; looking forward with much interest to my impartial verdict. On the subject of the women he was grave and spoke as follows:—

## Chapter X: The Woman Question

"When the Constitution was proclaimed, we thought it the millenium and imagined that the old restrictions were no longer needed. In the first days it really looked like that. We were all mad with freedom; Christians, Jews, Muslims embraced as brothers. Then all at once a thing occurred which brought us sharply back to face realities. A horrible event! You must have heard of it. Just over there, quite close to us. A Muslim girl, confiding in the shouts of liberty, married a Christian. Well, my friend, there was a rising. The pair were dragged out of their house and hacked to pieces in the open street. Worse than all that, there was a howl of satisfaction from the country, from the very women! We saw a hideous peril, to avoid which it was necessary to preserve indefinitely the rigorous seclusion of our Muslim women. There were no two parties at the time; all agreed on the necessity. The sole objectors were a section of the Christians who seemed to think we ought to anger and humiliate the Muslims for their sake. This matter of the women is the one point of fanaticism which still survives among us. The Government must consider the whole nation, not alone the few who have outgrown such prejudices. Remember that the ladies with whom you associate are quite exceptional, and might be murdered if they had the liberty which they desire."

He was quite right. And yet it seemed to me a pity that so much enthusiasm should have been repressed so bluntly, when an appeal to the unruly ladies upon grounds of patriotism, presenting them with an ideal and with work to do, might have done wonders for the party of reform. For Turkish women are intensely patriotic, and as a rule more energetic than the men.

## CHAPTER XI
# POLITICAL GOSSIP

The second armistice had been proclaimed and everyone believed the war was over. Officers on two or three days' furlough from Çatalca called on us, and Misket Hanum was surprised to find that her vituperation of the Bulgars was neither echoed nor applauded by these actual fighters. Their attitude towards the enemy was one of pure compassion. The Bulgars had, they told us, fought magnificently; their losses had been terrible, so great that they could hardly now be said to have an army. The capture of Adrianople had been their last great effort, which they never could have made successfully without the Serbs and Russian volunteers. A general told me that the Bulgars had petitioned for the armistice, and as soon as it was granted came in hundreds to the Turkish lines to beg for food. He said it made him downright sick to see the way the starving soldiers fell upon the food when it was given to them. The Bulgars had behaved like savages in Thrace and Macedonia; but that was the doing, he considered, chiefly of irregulars, whom it was always dangerous to use in Eastern warfare. That the massacres had been a definite part of the plan of campaign he verily believed, judging from the field left free to these irregulars, and from the fact that none of them, so far as he could learn, had yet been hanged, which would have been their fate in any civilised army. Of the regulars he spoke as he had found them— brave, fine troops, but utterly exhausted, in spite of all their claim to victory. They had beaten out their life on the Çatalca forts. Being thus weak, they would be pounced on by their own allies, as wolves devour the wounded leader of the pack. The Turks had now a well-appointed army in the field, compared with which the remnant of the Bulgar host, which at the outset of the war had been a splendid fighting force, was pitiful. As a soldier who had seen their army in its prime and much admired it, he could not but feel sorry for its utter ruin. This was the view of every Turkish soldier that one met. In our village, on the Asiatic shore of Marmara, life speedily resumed its normal flow.

There had been no festivities, public or private, among Muslims since October; but now one heard the gossip of a hundred weddings; and pleasure-trips and parties were once more allowed. Amid the social bustle which ensued I made a lot of new acquaintances, and heard some compliments upon my Turkish, which was getting fluent. Besides the khôja who came daily to instruct me and the talk of Misket Hanum and the servants, I had another most efficient teacher in the person of a neighbour's little boy, one Mehmet, who led me forth each morning to inspect the world. He would chatter away gaily, taking my intelligence for granted, then suddenly pull up before some object and demand: "What is it? Name its colour! Is it hard or soft? Animal, vegetable or mineral?" and so on. This duty towards me he performed with most impressive gravity, taking great pains with my pronunciation, which he said was grossly Arab. Sometimes an older boy, his cousin, sometimes a whole group of children bore us company when conversation soon became a little heated,, which passers-by observed with sympathetic grins. It was curious to hear these Turkish children, though quite intimate, address each other formally as "Bey Effendi!" "Hanum Effendi!" just like grown-up persons. This was the invariable custom formerly, but now the proper name is gaining ground; and a shout of "Mehmet!" "Safet!" or "Halil!" from one child to another is no longer thought ill-mannered.

Through little Mehmet I acquired a deal of nursery lore, of which my hostess was, I found, a great repository. She knew the language of the frogs, of many birds, and even plants, for we have seen her charm a little seed-pod of the crane's-bill with the words: "Dun, dun, babajik! Dunmasan kefani kesarim kanli kuyuya atarim!" (Turn, turn, little father! If you don't I'll break your head and throw you in the bloody well!) The seed-pod turned in evident alarm, to the admiration of myself and Mehmet, the more so that we tried and failed to work the marvel. Mehmet had a tenderness for all that lives. He had been known to weep most bitterly for fowls of his acquaintance when these appeared before him in the form of food. Walking with me in the garden, he would shriek suddenly and dance with anguish, tugging at my arm.

"You're treading on them!" he would cry. "The living ants!" He was not a strong child and from this and other indications I judged him something of a milksop. I was much mistaken. While I was learning Turkish from him, he on his side was employed demurely on a comprehensive study of my abnormalities. A born mimic, he soon acquired a perfect imitation of my strut, my frown, my grin, my tricks of gesture; these he adopted in his admiration for me, which, however, I discovered was by no means blind.

One day, when running, he fell down on a sharp stone and cut his knee, which bled profusely. I took him to my room and washed the cut, and generally made more fuss about the matter than I should have done had he impressed me as less frail. He looked surprised at first, which I set down to shock, and never cried at all; but, seeing my concern, screwed up his face to an expression of great agony, looked up at me with huge, pathetic no eyes and moaned "Neh kadar âjiyor!" (How much it hurts!) at intervals. When we went out again he limped alarmingly, requiring my support at every step. This lasted till his mother came in in search of him. She asked what was the matter. The boy was speechless owing, as it seemed, to pain. An accident? Yes, he had fallen down and cut his knee. The lady slipped aside the bandage I had made, glanced at the place and forthwith slapped it hard. She said he was a very naughty boy. To my surprise he did not thereupon dissolve in tears, but gave a skip, and, grinning in my face, exclaimed, "Neh kadar âjiyor!" in open mockery. It seemed he had been merely playing up to me in pursuance of his course of study of my character. I ought to have remembered that no Turk, whether man, woman, or child, has ever known that nervous shudder which most English people feel at the sight of blood. No matter whether it be their own or another's, no matter what the quantity, blood flowing is for the Turk a mere natural phenomenon, interesting only in so far as it can be prevented. This peculiarity has gained for them a name for callous cruelty, unjustly, for they are as kind as we are. The trait is one of fatalism, not of inhumanity. An important personage once condescended to describe to me the old-fashioned Turkish view of massacres, for instance. He said :—

"Here am I sitting in my room. They come and tell me there is killing going on outside. I tell them: Stop it instantly! They go, then come again, and say they cannot stop it. I then go out myself and view the matter and estimate the force at my disposal to put down the killing. If I find it insufficient or see clearly that my forces will betray me and go over to the crowd, thus ending my authority, I send for reinforcements. Suppose they do not come. I let the crimes go on, while taking careful note of the chief criminals, who have refused to hear me, reserving my authority for the punishment of the offenders afterwards, which punishment, I promise you, shall be exemplary." This method, though opposed to our ideas, possesses merits. But I have wandered far away from my friend Mehmet. The said Mehmet's parents, approving strongly of the friendship, made me free of their kiosk and their society. His mother was a very energetic, charming lady who sallied forth each day as a black shrouded phantom—unrecognisable until she spoke—on errands hardly consonant with the accepted English view of Turkish women. She had organised collections for the wounded, expeditions of food and tobacco to the front, had stood for hours with her adherents at the railway station in the bitter days of winter, amid sleet and snow, throwing gifts by handfuls into each compartment of the trains which passed in quick succession bringing soldiers up from Konia and Angora. At present she was organising a still greater work—a league of Turkish ladies for the patronage of Turkish industries. Her husband, a permanent official of high standing, was one of the most subtle thinkers it has ever been my luck to meet. His views of European politics, which he had studied more minutely than those of his own country—a failing of the modern Turk, as I have hinted—were singularly shrewd and, being quite impartial, fresh to me; and that his opinion upon Turkish matters was worth more than most men's. I gathered from the fact that, though an ardent Liberal, he sometimes had a good word for the Unionists. The other Liberals of our acquaintance were such bitter partisans that they had lost the will and the capacity to sit in judgment. "We are finished," they would mutter, "thanks to Europe, but chiefly thanks to those atrocious Unionists. Our shame is great. What must the French and English think of us, seeing us submit to the dominion of such men. If the earth would only open and engulf us!"

I have heard these friends of mine accuse the Unionists of every crime from petty theft to murder and incendiarism, and should probably have given credence to the charges had they been made general and not specifically aimed at persons whom I knew and liked. In order to explain the ground of this extremely bitter party feeling, I here give an outline of the history of the present Turkish parties. At the Revolution everyone became a Unionist either by conviction or from policy. There was in appearance no reactionary spirit; yet nine months later there broke out a counter-revolution in the form of a mutiny of the garrison of Constantinople. This mutiny has been ascribed to the personal intrigues of Abdul Hamid II., but seems rather to have been the work, without his knowledge, of those who owed to him a rank and fortune which they feared to lose under the new regime. It was quickly suppressed; the Young Turk army under Mahmud Shevket Pasha marched from Salonika and re-took the capital, which it entered amid scenes of wild enthusiasm; and once more everyone became a Unionist in outward seeming, though secret discontent prevailed among the upper classes. If there were men of sense and genuine patriotism on the Committee, there were also firebrands, whose arrogance offended the old notables. The various attacks upon the Empire more or less concerted by the Powers of Europe, which followed close upon the Revolution, were attributed by many to the new regime.

The Hamidian statesmen and officials, whose policy had been all outward deference towards the Powers, were horrified at the crude methods of the Young Turk Government, its callow trust in diplomatic protestations, its neglect of backstairs opportunities, espionage and little subsidies, of which the tyrant had availed himself with such success. The kinglets of Balkans found their incomes much reduced, so did the Albanian chiefs, so also, I have heard, did other personages belonging to a world reputed much more civilised. In Abdul Hamid's time a man could be a general in the army at twenty-one by influence. There were many youths thus foisted into high appointments. The reformers had them all examined and degraded to the rank for which they seemed designed by nature. Ministers who had preyed upon the country and grown rich were made to yield a portion of their spoils. The disarming of the Albanian mountaineers appeared untimely and was said to be performed in much too harsh a manner. But it was an attempt to centralise the Empire on a German plan, forcing the Turkish language upon all its races, even the proud Arabs, which gave the Opposition heart and popularity; though its leaders also made political capital out of the succession of disasters, culminating in the war with Italy, which had befallen the country under Unionist rule. The Liberals came into power in the summer of 1912 and formed what looked like a strong Ministry. They blame the Unionists for the disaster of the first part of the war, accusing them of having demoralised the army by sacrificing discipline to their political propaganda. The Unionists, on the other hand, contend that they had as much improved the army in the article of efficiency as in those of food and clothing, and ascribe the whole fiasco to the change made in its arrangements by the Liberals from party spite, and particularly to the madness of the Government in disbanding the army of Macedonia, at the instance of the Powers, when war was actually in sight.

On this last point the Liberals reply that they received a definite assurance from the Powers that no attack on Turkey by the Balkan States would be permitted. On that assurance they disbanded the said army, confiding in the honour of the Powers. "Why," the Unionists exclaim, "confide in something which they knew full well did not exist?" The Liberals admit that they would not have trusted Russia, but they trusted England. However that may be, the disbanding of a disciplined and well-tried army of 120,000 men just then was fatal in its consequences to the Turks. The men had just had time to scatter to their homes in distant provinces when war broke out; and to replace them irregulars and raw recruits were driven in. Some of these knew so little of a soldier's business that on the word of command: "At!" they all threw down their rifles, the same word meaning "Fire!" and also "Throw!" I have the story from an officer who had to do with them. Whether competent or no, the Liberal regime was a complete fiasco. Popular sentiment soon turned against a party whose accession to power had seemed the signal for calamity, and the community at large was not indignant when it fell in the little revolution of January, 1913? on which occasion Nazim Pasha lost his life. Here again the party versions are irreconcilable. The Liberals declare that Nazim's murder was premeditated. The Unionists protest that it was nothing of the kind, but rather pardonable homicide, committed in hot blood, and on the strongest provocation. I incline to take the latter view, and for this reason, that I never heard of any Turk who killed a man, as he imagined, for his country's good, who did not glory in the deed. That the Unionists express regret for Nazim's death seems to me proof positive that it was not included in their forecast of the January revolution.

In either case, it was a most unfortunate event, since it made the Liberals regard the Shevket Pasha Government with actual hatred. My Liberal friends assured me, now the war was ended, it would not be long before they overthrew those criminals and hanged them all. Allowing something for the Oriental vigour of imagination, I had heard such talk at home from eager partisans, so did not attach much importance to it. I was wrong in this, as will appear hereafter.

## CHAPTER XII
# A CONSPIRATOR

One afternoon I had been playing with Mehmet and some other children in the chestnut grove when a very dignified and handsome gentleman of thirty-five or thereabouts came towards us down the path from the house. Smiling upon my heated state indulgently but with the look of one who could not understand such levity of conduct in a grown-up person, he begged the favour of some private talk with me. Accordingly, I ushered him indoors, to Misket Hanum's little drawing-room, of which he shut the door—a most unusual course of action—before confiding to me: "In a very few days now, the Unionist Government will be overthrown for ever. There must be slaughter, but it will be no more than what is absolutely necessary—about five hundred persons who are really dangerous. It will not take a day to finish the whole work, all being well prepared. Then we shall carry out our great scheme of reform, part of which, relating to the Arab provinces, I have come to lay before you for your judgment."

These dreadful words were uttered in the soft low tone of voice which every Turk employs in ceremonious talk. The confidence with which he prophesied the speedy downfall of the Government amid more bloodshed, the way he seemed to gloat upon the prospect, made me sick at heart; for nothing more disastrous for the Ottoman Empire than another revolution at that juncture could have been devised by the most bitter enemy of Islam. How could this man, who evidently loved his country, fail to see that any government was better for that country now than any change? However, I did not betray my feelings, but simply asked in the same soft, purring tone which he had used, to hear the famous project of reforms. He then embarked upon a lengthy explanation, of which the details have escaped my memory. It was a scheme of "devolution" such as Mr Asquith might have fathered. There was to be a separate Parliament for Syria; another for Mesopotamia, and another, if I remember rightly, for, of all the regions of the earth, the great peninsula of Arabia with its thousand warring tribes and principalities. These countries would become at once autonomous, like English colonies, united only by allegiance to the Sultan, who would, of course, be represented by the Governors. What did I think of it? the visitor inquired, with a bright look of triumph, making sure of my approval.

I found it difficult to give polite expression to my thoughts of it. "But there is no demand for the breaking up of the Turkish Empire," was my answer, "and if there were, you would do wisely to oppose it."

"But our plan is to preserve the Empire, by making all the provinces contented."

"In fact, to run the school without the master!"

"By no means! Rather to unite free members of a league by ties of common interest."

"You have first to find, or educate, free members of your league."

## Chapter XII: A Conspirator

"But there is a demand for autonomy in those countries."

"Which reaches you by way of Paris, is it not so? If only the Turks would go themselves and study the condition of the Arab provinces, instead of accepting the opinion of their proven enemies, they would evolve some practicable scheme instead of mere Utopias!"

"But our scheme is better than the mad Unionist one of making all the Arabs into Turks. We are for decentralisation. It is the first need of the Empire."

The first need of the Empire, in my humble judgment, was the study of plain facts instead of airy theories, and the application to that study of a little common sense. The Unionists had thrown away their centralising scheme, and at last were giving due attention to the actual problem. The Liberals would have to throw away their theory of devolution and devote themselves to the same study, if they wished to keep those provinces within the Empire. I knew, I said, that I had earned the reputation of an Arab partisan by attacking Turkish indifference upon the subject of the Arab grievances whenever I could get a chance. But the Arabs seemed to me to be the hope of Turkey. Their mentality, if limited, possessed an energy and a directness which was lacking in the lazy greatness of the Turkish outlook. From heated arguments with certain Unionists, who wished to view them in the light of naughty children, I had retired despairing till a friendly word from Mahmud Shevket Pasha, carried to me by a friend, assured me that the rulers thought as I did.

At this my visitor smiled scornfully. He said: "They have deceived you. And even if they intend to do some good they will not have the opportunity, for they will soon be dead. Since you object to our treating the Arabs like children, and object to our treating them like full-grown men, what do you not object to, may I ask?"

I should have liked to see them treated on an equal footing with the Turks; to see both Turks and Arabs reinstated in that measure of self-government which was theirs under the early Sultans, before encroachments of the central power corrupted and destroyed the local checks upon administration provided by the laws of Islam. In a word, the communal and municipal institutions which still survived in name, ought to be made efficient and responsible. The chief fault of Turkish administration of late years had been its tendency to view the provinces as a species of gold mine, extracting all it could from them without return.

"All that you wish to see would happen naturally under the scheme which we propose," he answered lightly. Taking Syria for example, I asked to know his views upon the subject of the discontent reported from those provinces. He spoke of French intrigue in Beirut and the Lebanon, German and Jewish interests in Palestine, and seemed to think he had accounted for the whole of it. But those intrigues affected only the Christian population, which upon the whole was more contented than the Muslim, as I pointed out. When it was known that the Turks were being beaten in the war the Muslim population had gone so far as to express a wish for Syria to be annexed to Egypt. Why? Because they thought the Turks were finished, and with the Turks the Muslim Empire for the moment. And why should they have chosen to go under British rule rather than French or German? Because for many years there had been preached among them the Gospel of an Arab Empire under the Khedive. The Egyptians were unwarlike and above all lacked initiative. They would never, of themselves, throw off the British yoke; which, besides, was lighter than the yoke of other Powers, and did not crush, but rather fostered, independence in the subject. If a host of fiercer Arabs came beneath it for a time, sharing its gall and its good discipline, in a very little while a great explosion would take place, and European rule would cease in Western Asia and North Africa. But the Syrian Muslims were Muslims first, and Arabs afterwards. They would have died rather than desert in a bad day a Muslim Power which had treated them with

## Chapter XII: A Conspirator

due consideration. But when they saw the Turks defeated—finished, as they thought—they felt no obligation to adhere to them. The Turkish rule, for many years, had meant oppression tempered only by neglect.

"But our plan would remedy all that. Having a Parliament, they would control their own affairs."

"A Parliament! A water-melon!" I cried out, exasperated. "In Syria you have at least a hundred different tribes and interests, always embroiled and generally on the verge of war. The only way to keep them quiet is to keep them separate, and this at least the Turkish rule has done, or tried to do. Put Circassian and Bedawi, Durzi and Maruni, Beyruti and Shâmi, Orthodox and Catholic together in one Parliament, without the Turkish power to overawe them, and nothing under Allah could prevent a mêlée. Put all notions of separate Parliaments clean out of your head and give your close attention to the Arab provinces; establish order, study to ensure prosperity and educate! Educate! Educate! the people there and in the Turkish provinces in the duties and responsibilities of free citizenship which can only be done by giving them control of matters which immediately concern them. Encourage them to organise and carry out the public works required in their own towns and villages, tribes and communities, subject only to inspection by the central government."

"Another Utopia," laughed my visitor, when he had finished taking notes.

He then proposed that we should take a walk together. Accordingly we went down to the sea, and sitting on a ruined wall talked amicably until sunset. A man of European education, yet an ardent Muslim—the first I had encountered among Liberals—he proved a most agreeable companion. He had been in England for some years in Abdul Hamid's time, having been exiled like so many others, for no reason. One man I know was sentenced to imprisonment for life for having said once in the presence of a spy: "I am sick of this wretched country." Another was sent out with a whole class of military cadets, who had appealed to the Sultan against some new regulation in their school, in a bottomless boat to be drowned at sea, a fate from which they escaped by bribing the executioners and promising them never to return to Turkey while Abdul Hamid reigned. Men so ill-used became the enemies of their oppressor naturally, and hailed the revolution with delight. What I cannot explain, unless by supposing that conspiracy may become a habit as inveterate as drink or gambling, is that so many of them in a short while became conspirators against the new regime.

"It is a sad thing for a man to have to own that he has been mistaken," my companion sighed, gazing at the mountain islands bathed in sunset light. "The tyranny I loathed was less abominable than this so-called freedom. Still one must not despair. One must endeavour to destroy each fresh iniquity. Abdul Hamid was cruel and oppressed us, but he did keep out the foreigners, whom our present pack of rascals would receive with open arms. He had at least intelligence. Please God in three weeks' time these criminals will have received their wages, and the Empire will be saved. We have an understanding with the Russians, who are not so bad as people think. We shall be able to secure the country peace for a few years."

The man's sincerity was evident. But the word of trust in Russia, that immemorial foe of Turkish progress, showed the magnitude of his delusion. To have a free progressive Turkey on her frontiers, apart from Orthodox tradition and hereditary policy, could never be the wish of a despotic Russia; Russia had subsidised the tyrant and supported him for years. Russia would now, as always, give her aid to the reactionaries. Yet my poor friend, while boasting her support, believed himself a true progressive. I tried to make him see that what his country needed was not more revolution, but a stable Government. He answered:

## Chapter XII: A Conspirator

"We cannot have that till these rogues have been exterminated." One little point in his behaviour greatly pleased me. Although he had put his personal safety in my hands, although he knew I was in constant touch with Unionists, he never asked me to regard our conversation as in confidence. When a few days later I chanced to hear that the police were after him, it was the remembrance of that very gentlemanlike omission which made me for a moment quit my chosen standpoint of the mere observer. But I did not at the time regard him as a very serious conspirator; so like was he in talk and manner, even in appearance, to patriots one sometimes hears in English clubs expatiating on Lloyd George and other nuisances: "The country won't stand it, sir. The fellow'll get shot, and serve him right."

In the case of Englishmen one associates such speech with the reverse of action, and the superficial likeness of the Turks to Englishmen is so remarkable as in itself to be sufficient to mislead a man who has been used to Arabs. I tried, however, to impress upon my Liberal friends the inadvisability of any move on their part at a time when European opinion was turning round in favour of the Turks. Another revolution, marked by bloodshed, would make all Europe view the Turks as hopeless. "Why will they not understand," one man to whom I spoke thus cried despairingly, "that we are still in revolution? How long did France take to evolve a stable Government? And why are they so horrified at bloodshed? It is sometimes needed. As a people we are more law-abiding than any in Europe; there is much less crime here in proportion to the population than there is in England. It is only where our country and religion are concerned that we are ruthless. Show me another way to purge the State of malefactors."

They all accused me of a total lack of understanding, and I threw back the accusation flatly; so we got no further. Meanwhile my wife arrived from England. The flutter consequent on that event, the visits, counter-visits and unbounded kindness of the Turks of both opinions, had thrust politics into the background, when all at once there came the tidings that the Grand Vizier had been assassinated.

CHAPTER XIII
# THE ELEVENTH OF JUNE

On the 29th of May (old style) I had gone up after luncheon to write letters in a room which, being on the shady side of the house and further sheltered by the deodars, remained comparatively cool amid the noonday blaze, when Misket Hanum rushed in without ceremony and, collapsing on the sofa, burst out sobbing:

"They have murdered Mahmud Shevket— five men— fifty bullets. What wickedness! Mr Okapian has just come with the news."

She was completely overcome, incapable of a connected narrative. My wife came in to sit with her while I went down to interview the bearer of the tidings. This was the husband of an Armenian lady who, with her daughter, had been with us for some days. I found the three of them in the small drawing-room, their faces indicative of extreme concern, for they were Unionists. The man, it seemed, had but that day returned from Egypt, where he had a business. Arriving in the middle of the morning, he had been surprised to find his flat at Pera empty, and, hearing that his wife had gone to Misket Hanum's, set off at once to fetch her. Having some time to wait for the next steamer at the Bridge, he had looked into the Bourse at noon, and there had heard the news of the assassination of the Grand Vizier, which meant, he thought, another revolution.

Mahmud Shevket Pasha had been going from the Ministry of War to the Sublime Porte, as his custom was at eleven o'clock each morning, when, in the open space before the Mosque of Sultan Bayazid his car was forced to draw up to let something pass. At once, as at a signal, certain men who had alighted from another motor car sprang on to the steps and fired on him at close quarters. An aide-decamp who flung himself across his chief was killed at once; the Grand Vizier expired some twenty minutes later in the lobby of the Ministry of War. The assassins had made good their escape, and were doubtless now engaged on other murders as disastrous to the State. He (the narrator), having heard the news, had come straight on to Misket Hanum's to bring home his wife and daughter.

I suggested that the news might possibly prove false, to give some comfort to the women; but, remembering my talk with the conspirator that evening by the sea, I had no doubt but that a revolution was in progress. The wickedness of internecine strife at such a time, when Turkey needed all the strength of all her men; the devilish wantonness of killing Mahmud Shevket, the one man of his party who must, one would have thought, by all men be regarded as superior to party hate, the most hard-working and sincere of patriots, lightly, as men kill a noxious beast, made me, a lover of the Turks, feel downright ill.

A little later in the afternoon, at three o'clock, a noise of firing from the direction of the city gave us all a thrill; but a Turkish gentleman who called about that time assured us that the sound we heard was but the ordinary cannon practice, of which the customary notice had been given in the morning's papers. We did not quite believe him at the time, though it

## Chapter XIII: The Eleventh of June

relieved our minds to know that anyone could think that things were going on as usual.

This Turkish visitor, although a Unionist and a great partisan of Mahmud Shevket, was much more philosophical than we were. Indeed, his chief distress appeared to be on our account, that we should take the incident so much to heart. He agreed with me that the assassination of a man so useful would be senseless and a great disaster to the country, and hoped with me that the report was false. In hope to learn the truth at once he sent off one of the gardeners with a note to the district chief of the police, who was a friend of his. The answer he received, I well remember, was: "It is a thing you must not ask" (Sormamali bir shey dir). But when my wife and Misket Hanum spoke in pity of the murdered man, he differed gently from them. "When one is Grand Vizier one must expect to be assassinated," he said, smiling, and went on to proclaim the beauties of a sudden death. Death was as natural as life. It came to everybody. Why should that individual be pitied, to whom it came in swift and easy form? If one believed, as he supposed we all did, in a future state where virtue meets reward the man who died thus in his country's service, working for the Faithful, should be envied. He was evidently puzzled by my attitude, which lacked philosophy, and concerned at the deep sorrow of the women, whom he strove by coaxing methods to bring back to smiles.

As it happened I had promised for that afternoon to call upon a friend at a distance who was kept indoors by illness. In the excitement I forgot this duty until rather late, and went at last with mind intent upon apologies. The man whom I was going to visit was, I knew, a Liberal, but so polite and kindly that I felt assured that he would share my feelings on the tidings of this murder. I had made up my mind, however, not to speak of it since it disgraced his party, when as I walked up through the garden to the house his little girl called out to me in glee:

"Have you heard the news? Mahmud Shevket Pasha! Fifty bullets in him! They did well! "The child put up her hand as if it held a pistol and made "Click!" with her tongue repeatedly.

I cried: "For shame! They did extremely ill. It is possibly the end of Turkey, do you understand?"

She cried out: "Mother! Come and listen! The English Bey says Mahmud Shevket's killing is the end of Turkey!"

Her mother then came round the corner of the house, and eyed me with the sort of gloating smile which I have seen upon the countenance of Arab boys when torturing some bird or beast in order to get money out of tourists. She triumphed in her own immunity from what I felt.

"The end of Turkey?" she said superciliously, in French, quizzing me the while from half-closed eyes. "I hardly think so! Turkey, I fancy, will survive the death of that! If you are so upset by this small matter, what will you be tomorrow when you hear that hundreds of that canaille have been killed?"

I was going to reply when the master of the house appeared and bade me welcome in sardonic tones. He ushered me indoors into the great reception room, where I found a Jew or an Armenian, I cannot say which, since the man's name was not mentioned in my presence, in the seat of honour— an evil-looking, black-browed, hook-nosed man with predatory eyes. To this personage I was presented, with a mocking laugh as, "Monsieur Pickthall, le fameux Unioniste." The tone my host employed throughout the interview was downright rude to me. But I could not hold him quite responsible for what he said, since it was evident that he was wildly agitated. He could not keep still a moment, but kept striding off to the remotest corners of the room, returning to discharge some fresh offence at me. I believe that the Armenian visitor—he must, I think, have been an Armenian, for the Jews are almost wholly of the Young Turk party—was a hanger-on of the conspiracy. In all the passionate disastrous quarrels of the Turks there is a Christian somewhere, playing Mephistopheles, as it would

## Chapter XIII: The Eleventh of June

seem, from pure and simple love of mischief for its own sake. At any rate he had just come with news of the assassination. He gave me a few details that I had not heard before, as that what caused the stoppage of the Grand Vizier's motor-car was a Muslim funeral.

"They suspect that it was not a real funeral," put in our host with mock solemnity, and then went off into another of his nervous laughs. "However that may be, this mighty personage is dead—as dead as Nazim! Do you understand?"

The Armenian then, to change the subject, seeing I disliked it—inquired politely whether I enjoyed my stay in Turkey. I forget exactly what my answer was; but, whatever it was, it brought my host back in a flash from the far corner of the room. He came close, but did not confront me, while he cried:

"You make all this fuss about the man they have just killed! Was he anything to you? Was he a friend of yours? Did you know him at all well? Have you a clear idea what sort of man he was?"

He then began to pour abuse upon the character of Mahmud Shevket Pasha, vowing that he spoke from knowledge of the man. I suppose my listening face betrayed disgust, for the Armenian, who was watching me with his hawk eyes, said softly:

"I perceive that you are disappointed in the Turks."

His smile, and a slight shrug his shoulders gave, appeared to be directed at our host in some derision.

I had borne the rudeness of the latter calmly, for it was obviously the outcome of deep feeling. His agitation and bad temper were indeed more sympathetic to me than had been the light philosophy of the Unionist Turk whom I had left at Misket Hanum's. He was a friend of mine, and I could see that his offensive tone proceeded from annoyance that I should have seen him thus thrown off his balance. The man at any rate possessed a conscience which tormented him for some small share that he had had in the conspiracy. His rudeness could not fill me with the deep disgust I felt at the attempt of that Armenian, a bad angel of the Turks, to claim a fellow-feeling with me.

"Not altogether; but I hate their parasites," or something of that sort was my reply. Therewith I rose to go. The master of the house was just then saying that the incident of which I chose to make so great a fuss was really of but very small importance. He tried a careless laugh. I said that, as I was no Turk, I could not take a cheerful view of public crimes. I regarded them as so much stupid, brutal, useless sacrifice of lives whose value to the country at that moment was inestimable.

"As for useless, we shall see!" he answered from set teeth. "At this moment, it may be that the Unionist Government has fallen never to rise again." Then, breaking sharply off, he added: "Oh, you English! How can you understand what we endure? I have always said that French and English people are too far off from us to understand. You well-fed men, you blame the hungry malefactor!"

Everything in England, he declared, ran smoothly. There was a vast machine which worked almost of itself; the men were of but slight importance as compared with the machine; whereas in Turkey there was no machine, the men were everything. It was all personal. And law was not so well established and respected but that men who had a grievance, or ideal, killed for it. While he was declaiming thus, I bowed to the Armenian, saluted him and marched out. The lady of the house—a delicately pretty woman— and her little girl were still in the same place beneath a bower of banksia roses which just then caught the colour of the sunset.

"You know what is going on there now," she cried at my approach, stretching out her arm towards Stamboul, in which direction a hill with some fantastical kiosks upon it stood up in silhouette against the setting sun.

"Stop and listen for one minute!" the small child called out. "They did well, I do assure you, to kill Mahmud Shevket."

"Wait till tomorrow! You will think of this as nothing then!" her mother sent behind me with a merry laugh.

## Chapter XIII: The Eleventh of June

My friends had changed beyond all recognition. From highly civilised people they had turned to savages, in a moment, at the scent of a blood feud; for that was the true nature of the party struggle in their eyes. The savagery was Balkan, hardly Turkish. The Turkish attitude towards bloodshed is exemplified in the remark of our Unionist friend upon the tidings of the murder: "When one is Grand Vizier, one must expect to be assassinated. May God have mercy on him!" uttered with a pleasant smile. The Asiatic Turks are singularly unrevengeful for so brave a race. It is the European—chiefly the Albanian element, so strong among the richer classes—which calls for murder in the party strife.

Our little company was so depressed that evening that the Greek maid, in surprise, rebuked us, saying that the murder of a Turk was no such matter of concern. Her challenge failing to produce the usual argument, she felt alarm for our condition and advised us all to go to bed.

Few people, I imagine, in our village got a wink of sleep that night, for all believed a revolution would have taken place before the morning. As a lover of Islam, I was myself a prey to great anxiety, for the man who had been killed that day was the one man whom I knew to have the will and the capacity to save his country from the hundred enemies, inside and out, who threatened its existence, and so save Islam from undeserved humiliation and a consequent revival of fanaticism. If the Government held firm there might still be some hope; in case of revolution, which seemed then the far more probable event, the reactionaries would obtain the power, such as it was, and, hated as they were by the majority, would lean for their support on foreign governments, known enemies. The end might be deferred awhile but it was sure, in that case.

I leaned out of my window after midnight, listening in the direction of the city. But the task was hopeless, for the night was full of noises. It was bright as day with moonlight. Three nightingales were singing loudly close at hand, the frogs were quacking raucously around the lake; cocks were crowing, dogs were howling, and a bekji (watchman) in the distance was shrilling the accustomed cry of "Yanghin Vâr!" (There is a fire.) His cry drew nearer, and I then learnt that the fire in question was miles away, at Büyükdere, up the Bosphorus. Desirous as I was of catching sounds more distant—sounds of shooting —if any such were floating in the air, I was astonished by the volume of the common noises of the night, which seemed to me unusual and conscious. It was the perfect Turkish midnight of the poets. The shrouded trees were sighing to the moon. The nightingale kept shrieking to the rose "Gyul, Gyul, Gyul, Gyul, Achil, Achil, Achil!" (Rose, rose, rose, rose, open, open, open!) The frogs about the lake discussed their business also in Turkish words distinctly audible: "Omar Agha!" "Neh vâr ô?" "Burjum vâr!" "Ver da kurtul!" (Omar Agha!—Yes, what's the matter?—I am in debt.—Pay and get free!)

Gusts of perfume from the garden came and went. The few kiosks discoverable from my point of vantage showed lighted lattices. Their inmates had no thought of sleep that night. Beyond the furthest shapes discernible, a pearly horizontal gleam, a kind of netted radiance, marked the sea. Man's kingship over nature was an empty boast. The world belonged more truly to the frogs and nightingales who have, it may be, doubts of man's existence.

CHAPTER XIV

# ASSASSINATION AS A TONIC

Next morning, with the first sunlight, I was out walking in the maze of avenues which stretched between the village and the sea. The trunks of plane and mulberry trees red-stained in splashes by the sun's first rays, the mystery of their enormous shadows joined to the heavy rolling foliage, made of the suburban thoroughfares a sacred grove, the haunt of nymph and faun; while, beyond the twisted columns and the shade, the sea was visibly the sea which Jason sailed, the sea whose foam gave birth to Aphrodite. Strange as it may seem such classical illusions flourish in the atmosphere of Turkey rather than in that of modern Greece. A veiled and shrouded woman flitting under the trees from one garden-gate to another brought this home to me. She belonged to the unconscious, ancient world. The Turks preserve the old Greek's love of beauty for its own sake; his delight in seaside vistas, colonnades, white temples, solemn cypress-groves; his clear poetic gaze at love and death; whereas the modern Greek's romance is simply money.

I walked a mile or two along the Baghdad road to open country, between the purple mountains and the shore. The world was well astir, for Turks are early risers. Peasants with bullock waggons, laden mules or donkeys passed me, going into one or other of the landing-stages on the Bosphorus. A new white mosque among some trees inland attracting me, I made for it across the fields. A poetical inscription stated that it had been erected by a Pasha of the neighbourhood in memory of his beloved wife whose name it bore. It was a lovely temple in a lovely spot, but for the Anatolian railway running close at hand; and even that was more incongruous than ugly. A single line of metals ran along the middle of a broad rough road, busy with the morning traffic of the district, which road meandered among wooded gardens occupied by quaint kiosks. Men in bright coloured clothing, black and white veiled women, horses, sheep, and oxen moved upon it. Pursuing it in my way home I happened on a youth whom I knew slightly returning from the railway station, whither he had gone for news. He told me that the Government held firm.

All the Turkish papers at the station had been sold before the gardener, who went each day to buy one for us, got there. Therefore I heard no further details till I went to town. I started about ten o'clock, to find, on my arrival in Stamboul, that the state funeral accorded to the Grand Vizier was over. It had been, I was assured, a most imposing ceremony, attended by the representatives of all the Powers, followed and watched by patriotic crowds. One of the assassins, Topal Tevfik (lame Tevfik), had been caught, they told me, and the police were confident of laying hands on all the others. The humble funeral, for which the Grand Vizier had stopped his car, had been proved, upon investigation, to be genuine, the men who led it absolutely ignorant of any plot. The conspirators had drawn up their car beside the public fountain on one side of the square of Sultan Bayazid, meaning to run it out and block the way for Mahmud Shevket's motor. The appearance in the nick of time of a funeral procession, filling up a street made narrow by some building operations then in progress, removing the necessity for this manoeuvre, they had jumped out and run the few steps necessary in order to fire point blank at their victim. Having achieved their object, they had scurried back and set off in the motor at a furious pace, attracting general notice—a fact which was of signal help to the police in their researches—all except Topal Tevfik, who, being lame and consequently slower than the rest, was left behind. He limped back to the tavern where he lodged, and was arrested there a few hours later. The scene of the assassination was the space immediately before the mosque of Sultan Bayazid, known to tourists as the "pigeon mosque," whose cloister is among the glories of Stamboul.

Walking about the streets, I found them just as usual, except that the patrols were doubled, and that here and there at points of vantage troops were picketed. The business of the town proceeded just as usual. It struck me, I remember, as remarkable, that neither in my going or my coming, did I meet a single Liberal of my acquaintance. When I remarked to a man, who came and talked to me, upon the absence of some notable from his accustomed place, he laughed and said:

"They are all in it, from Kiamil Pasha, that high pattern of respectability beloved of England, to miserable hangers-on like Topal Tevfik. Well, they have brought it on themselves; they had their warning. You remember what a fuss was made when Kiamil Pasha was forbidden to remain here. Many people thought it hard on the old man; but Jemâl Bey had certain information, and he warned them then."

He added gravely that the danger was by no means over, which seemed to be the general opinion. A group of military cadets with whom I travelled on the homeward boat, were in a state of wild excitement and anxiety. They had all been to the funeral of Mahmud Shevket. Most of them had known the blessed martyr (as they called him) personally in his capacity as Minister of War; and their cry was all for vengeance on his murderers. "They have slain the best hope of our country," cried one youth, an Arab. "If they kill Talaat, Jemâl and a dozen more, as they propose, there will be no one left to guide and save the nation."

These young men, drawn from every quarter of the Turkish Empire, who, after eight or ten years' study in the capital, are once again dispersed throughout the different provinces, are a valuable asset of Young Turkey. Their rage on this occasion did me good. In Turkey one grows sometimes weary of resigned philosophy.

That evening as we sat at dinner, a messenger arrived with the news that certain of our neighbours wished to visit us at half-past eight o'clock. Pleasure was, of course, expressed on the announcement, but a good deal of embarrassment was felt by us, for the visitors were the young couple I had called upon the day before, the same who had betrayed such savage glee on hearing of the murder of poor Mahmud Shevket. We agreed, as far as might be, to keep conversation distant from the burning topic; began, I recollect, by laying out some French and German illustrated papers, of which Misket Hanum kept a store, to make material for conversation. But the pair, it proved, had come to talk of nothing else, resolved to have the matter out with me. They did not apologise for their behaviour of the previous day—I never knew a Turk whose pride would brook the notion of apology where one was seriously due—but they made concessions and decided overtures. The man and I embarked on a long argument which led at length to understanding though without agreement. I confessed that party madness was excusable considering the harassed state of Turkey, and he admitted in the end that it was undesirable, going so far as to describe both parties as "two clouds of greedy crows" intent upon the body politic. Our friendship, far from being weakened by the wrangle, was confirmed. "It remains, however, to be seen," he said at

## Chapter XIV: Assassination as a Tonic

parting, "whether the Unionists will be able to find men to fill the vacant places in the Ministry. Few men will choose to court assassination. They are to be pitied truly. All this bluster and parade of strength proclaims their weakness." But though the vacant posts were filled but slowly, I saw no sign of fear or weakness in the Government. One day when I was going into town by train there entered my compartment at a wayside station that same influential member of the Committee of Union and Progress who had shown me kindness in the matter of the Balkan massacres. He was one of the new ministers, a man marked out for murder. Yet he appeared as merry as a schoolboy. When I offered my felicitations to him, apologising for the word as hardly fitting in the circumstances, he laughed and said that someone must help carry on the government. At Haïdar Pasha where we all got out, I saw him beam to right and left, returning the salute of notables, clapping young men on the shoulder, his benevolent large face expressive of the highest glee.

That day I had been asked to luncheon by a friend and, landing at the Bridge, went straight to his abode. He hailed me with a jollity which seemed a little shocking in an intimate of Mahmud Shevket Pasha on that, the first occasion of our meeting since the sad event.

"Well," he inquired, "have you made up your mind about our parties yet? Can you now differentiate them and define them clearly?"

I said that I should call the Liberals the Cosmopolitan, the Unionists the Nationalist Turkish party; that the latter seemed to me to wish to raise the common people to intelligent participation in the work of government; while the former wished, without malevolence towards the subject people, to keep things pretty nearly as they were, securing their own status as the ruling class, and figuring as wardens of the Powers of Europe over savage hordes; but that the fierce reactionary attitude recently assumed by Liberals, in my opinion, put them out of court.

"Bravo!" he cried. "But what is your opinion of these last events? We have now got the lists of those to be assassinated. It is lengthy. The conspirators who bound themselves by oath to do the work are many. Most of them are still at large. But Jemâl Bey is wonderful. He has arranged things so that if they kill him and all the present leaders, government will still go on. A little disappointment for them—eh? The situation is both interesting and amusing."

My friend seemed strangely happy, and in better health than I had ever seen him, for he was generally something of an invalid. He, too, was on the list, I found out later. It really does exhilarate a man of feeling to have the complicated and distracting villainies behind him reduced to one plain issue for him—sudden death. To die is such an easy thing for man to do—the simplest thing of all, as Turks behold it.

CHAPTER XV

# THE MEN AND THE CAUSE OF THE CONSPIRACY

It was surprising, when I came to think of it, how many persons whom I used to meet continually had disappeared about the time of Mahmud Shevket Pasha's death, being summoned suddenly to Europe or to distant parts of Turkey. The Government had had an inkling of the plot for many weeks and Jemâl Bey, the "commandant de place" (governor of the city under martial law) had warned the ringleaders that they were being watched, which may account for some of those abrupt departures. But as the said Jemâl Bey was one of the first three dignitaries who were to have been murdered, the majority of the suspected laughed at him, believing that their plans were too well laid for failure. Indeed, the overweening confidence of the conspirators—without the least foundation, as it proved—is, psychologically, the most curious feature of the whole affair. For example, they sent notice to the foreign embassies that there would be a change of government on such a day, and asked that sailors might be landed to protect the Christian quarter; the idea behind this action being to create a panic favourable to their designs, which, they never seemed to doubt, were pleasing to the Powers of Europe.

That they had a little ground for this presumption is true; for the Russian and the British Embassies, especially, had in the past been hostile to the Young Turks, lending the weight of all their influence to Kiamil Pasha's party, of which the aim was to establish something like the old régime. More astonishing was the undoubtedly sincere belief of the conspirators that they were popular, and that the nation as a whole would welcome their return to power. They viewed themselves as saviours of their country and deemed their cause so plainly righteous that it must appeal to everyone. In point of fact they were detested by the common people, at any rate within a ten mile radius of the capital. During my stay in Turkey there were only two occasions when I noticed anything resembling public feeling, as we understand the term in England, that is, keen indignation shown by ordinary quiet people on political events—a phenomenon unknown in Muslim countries formerly, when public sentiment clung only to religious questions. One was the fall of Adrianople; the other the assassination of the Grand Vizier. I remember overhearing two of our Laz gardeners cursing some friends of ours well-known for Liberals. The head gardener was of opinion that they needed hanging much more than did Kyur Amin and Topal Tevfik (two of the assassins), poor men, mere instruments, whom such as they had bought with gold. He would have liked, he said, himself to drag them out of their fine house down to the village coffee-shop, where they might learn what honest people and good Muslims thought of them. The speaker wished the Government might take them all.

Each day we had the news of fresh arrests—in our own village there were five one morning—until the prisoners were numbered by the hundred. Pera was thrown into a panic by the noise of firing in her midst, a battle raging round a house of ill-repute where some of the conspirators had taken refuge; and complained a little that the Embassies did not prevent the Turks from making such a terrifying noise. But Pera is a rabbit-warren for pure nerves. The iron shutter of a shop fell down once in the main street at a busy hour, when in two minutes the whole street was empty, every door was barred. For long our Liberal friends retained a hope that the revolution would break out again and meet success. But their agents were outwitted and outmatched at all points. Not for a moment did the Government give way to terror, which they had counted on as their most powerful auxiliary. The murderers of Mahmud Shevket Pasha, the persons in the motor-car (the whole idea had evidently been borrowed from the motor-bandit incidents in Paris) would seem to have been terrified by their own deed, for they fled wildly, abandoning their further project, which had been to drive full speed to the Sublime Porte and, occupying the office of the Grand Vizier, to summon other victims in his name. The plan might have succeeded by its very daring had its execution been entrusted to whole-hearted men instead of hirelings. Had the criminals succeeded in the first five minutes in killing Mahmud Shevket Pasha, Jemâl Bay, and Tala'at Bey according to their hopes, they might have stopped authority for a time sufficient to allow them to make good their strength; but even that is doubtful, for the case had been foreseen. As it was, after the first five minutes they never had the least chance of success against a great commander such as Jemâl Bey. For days the hunt went on; men of all conditions were arrested; the documents of the conspiracy were found, among them a full list of members of the Kiamil Pasha party; and for once the envoys of the Powers forbore to intervene. I mention this, as it was much remarked among the Turks. My chief friend in the current of affairs considered it extraordinary. He said, he wished that someone would inform the British Government of the injury that had been done to British prestige in Constantinople by our

Embassy intriguing on its own account. When I asked to know precisely what he meant, he told me he referred particularly to intrigues upon behalf of Kiamil Pasha and his colleagues just before the Balkan war. All Turkey had, he said, been given to understand that Kiamil Pasha carried with him the support of England. The British Embassy had worked hard for Kiamil, and he must suppose that it had acted in this case without instructions from the British Government, since no support whatever was vouchsafed to the old man during his brief disastrous term of office. The Liberals, I knew as well as he did, felt still more bitterly than did the Unionists upon this subject, saying openly that they had been betrayed by England. He had nothing against Kiamil Pasha personally, he assured me, except that he was much too old for public business— a great deal older than he said he was—well over ninety. The country and the army would never have tolerated him nor the ministry of which he formed a part but for the belief which, as he said, appeared to have a good foundation, that he carried with him the support of England. That support meant more to Turks just then than party triumphs.

I have here put mildly, without comment, the purport of perhaps a dozen conversations.

Then came the trial by court martial of the host of prisoners. I thought that the actual murderers only should be put to death; but everybody laughed at my idea as weakness, and said a great example must be made. This was no common murder, I was asked to bear in mind. A number of wealthy influential persons had tried to overthrow the State at a time when special laws were, as they perfectly well knew, in force for its protection. It would be a sin to let them go, and punish hirelings only. This view was that of every Turk I knew who had no active sympathy with the conspirators. The death— or, as they called it, martyrdom—of Mahmud Shevket Pasha had alarmed the whole community, and quiet men, who had till then disowned both parties, were now Unionists.

## Chapter XV: The Men and the Cause of the Conspiracy

The contention, which I often heard from Liberals, that the deed was, taken at its worst, fair vengeance for the death of Nazim, was not endorsed by any Turk outside that party. Dire punishment was looked for, and it came. Some who had fled the country were condemned to death by default; many more were exiled; twelve were hanged. To show the value of a punishment which seemed to me excessive: a very peaceful, law-abiding Syrian merchant whom I know, being in Stamboul, went to see the bodies hanging on the gibbets, and touched one of them. He told the tale with placid satisfaction. "Then I felt more comfortable," he said, "for then I knew for certain that we had a government."

If I have dwelt at tedious length upon the state of parties in Constantinople, it is because false views are current on the subject. I myself was utterly misled, in England and elsewhere, by the account of men in a position to be perfectly informed thereof; and went to Turkey with a prejudice against the Unionists which obscured my judgment for the first three months. There is to be observed in Western Europeans generally a tendency to scoff at the bare thought of Eastern progress. But Eastern Europeans take a different view. They are alarmed lest Turkey should rise up in earnest. M. Miliukoff's reports of the reality of Turkish progress precipitated the late Balkan war. Again, the kind of progress contemplated by the Turks, and sanctioned by Muslim tradition, has a look of socialism terrifying to despotic Russia, and probably displeasing to all European governments. It is, therefore, natural that the young Turks should have been condemned by Europe; but let none imagine that the condemnation was in Turkey's interest.

The aim of all the opposition was to hinder an experiment, however interesting, which might encourage and excite the neighbouring peoples; and also to keep the Ottoman Empire in a condition to be presently divided up among its high protectors. For this reason, ever since the Revolution, the Powers have welcomed every symptom of reaction. It is only fair to add, however, that the Turkish party of reaction does not see all this; wholly absorbed as are its members in their own contentions as against the Unionists. While the nucleus of that party is compact of those who found their profit in the old régime, it includes some men of honestly progressive notions, who were disgusted by the early blunders of the Unionists, or whose sentiment had been offended by their brusque reforms. For example, the sad fate of the dogs of Constantinople made many people treat the men concerned as malefactors. I have heard it solemnly averred that the defeat of Turkey in the first part of the war was a judgment on the country for that act of cruelty. Men of some experience in state affairs saw posts for which they were themselves well fitted occupied by men of zeal but no experience, and were conscious of a danger to the country. The privileged class of Abdul Hamid's day enjoyed a high degree of luxury as well as freedom, at the Sultan's pleasure. Its homes were beautiful, its women often highly cultivated, while many of its members were familiar with the art and thought of Europe. They recognised no duty towards the people of the land, but only towards the Sultan in whose hands they were. Many of them were benevolent in private life, but in their public functions they were forced by their attachment to an evil system to consent to crimes. It is probable that most of them were truly thankful for the revolution when it came. There were aspects of the Hamidian dispensation which must have sickened everyone except a downright villain; and the perpetual fear, the need of circumspection, incidental to the service of the tyrant, could not but be irksome to ease-loving men. Had the revolution given them the liberty it seemed to promise, at the same time preserving the old pompous atmosphere they loved, and not attacked their fortunes or their rank, most of them would, I think, have been contented. It was they who, in the first days of the Constitution, were most eager to advance at once to European freedom. But liberty, as understood by the reformers,

## Chapter XV: The Men and the Cause of the Conspiracy

meant no advance on that which they had previously enjoyed; quite otherwise, for they were now no longer lords protected. For the first time they were exposed and in a sense subjected to the prejudices of the common people, whose ignorance gave law to their enlightenment. The Young Turks placed their whole ideal in the future, their present hope in education and reforms. The other party at its best desired no less the nation's welfare, but objected to the "men and brethren" tone of the Young Turks as demagogic and subversive of all order. The people had a proper place and should be kept there.

Eventually they were driven far from their original position by the necessity of opposing every project of the enemy. As an opposition, which of course was needed, they did good. Eighteen months ago they had secured a large share of popular sympathy. But their violence in opposition latterly outran their patriotism. To call the Young Turk rule a despotism more terrible than that of Abdul Hamid, is bosh, to use a common Turkish word. The change in Turkey for the better struck me as miraculous (though I visited the country in an hour of great disaster), more especially when I considered that the five years of the revolution had been years of war. It is that disturbance from without, preventing the revolution from working out to a decided end, and especially the intrigues of foreign governments against the new regime, which caused the furious state of party feeling which I have described. In brief, it is the fault of Europe, first and last. Europe with its accustomed nervous dread of popular upheaval, regarded the Young Turks as upstarts, insolently bullying an aristocracy, their natural rulers. If the Hamidian guard of high officials and their hangers-on, picked as they were from any quarter at the tyrant's pleasure, can by any means be called an aristocracy, it was truly the most upstart and the least efficient that the world has ever seen. Upon the other hand the Turkish nation altogether may be fairly regarded as an aristocracy—the aristocracy of the whole Muslim world. As such it is efficient and invaluable, deserving the entire support of any Power which has at heart the peace and welfare of the East.

In periods of history such as that the Turks have just been traversing, men feel unsettled and resent the feeling; and their resentment sometimes takes the form of madness. With peace, the insane bitterness would soon subside, as people grew accustomed to the new conditions. The men who plotted to destroy the Turkish Government, who murdered Mahmud Shevket, and were hanged or exiled, were no worse than any of our English politicians of today, except in that they lived in maddening times and were prepared to risk their lives for their opinions.

## CHAPTER XVI
# THE ARMY OF THE WEST

One afternoon, upon the terraced ground in front of Misket Hanum's house, shaded and screened from observation by the deodars, a Turkish lady who was sitting with us all at once exclaimed, "What noise is that?" turned deathly pale and seemed about to faint. The noise referred to was a shout or roar such as one hears in England at a football match, but so far distant that it had escaped the notice of the rest of us. It was repeated, when we knew it for the "Padishahim chôk yasha!" (Long live the Sultan) which Turkish troops upraise on great occasions. We had heard it often in the last few days.

"Oh, horrible!" whispered our visitor, stopping her ears. "It is the Army of the West! Poor souls! I cannot bear it. Forgive my weakness. Let us go indoors!"

She was the still youthful widow of a Turkish general (by birth an Arab) who had been assassinated in Albania the land from which the Army of the West—all that remained of it—had just returned. We went indoors, and she recovered quickly, begging us to overlook her foolishness. She would not have us, for the world, imagine that Turkish women had no fortitude. But her grief had been revived that day by tidings that the Government intended to bring home her husband's body from the distant land where it was buried for reinterment with the heroes of the Constitution upon the Hill of Everlasting Liberty. And the shout just now had come so suddenly, reminding her of that Albania which had caused so much disaster to the Turks, that it had struck her heart. The condition of the Army of the West, she said, was terrible beyond conceiving.

On the following day two students from the Army Medical School took luncheon with us, and in the afternoon a fine white-bearded Turk—a famous poet and a senator—surprised us with a visit. The young men told with glee the story of a riot at their school upon the previous day. When the first instalment of the Army of the West was disembarked at Haïdar Pasha, the garden near the Medical School was used for a camp hospital, and the students were required to go and help in it. Our two informants clenched their teeth, their eyes flashed fiercely, as they spoke of the condition of the soldiers. Many were demented or had lost their memory; but those who could speak had related, uncomplainingly, a tale of such cold-blooded cruelty from so-called Muslims to their Muslim brothers as sent the blood of all the students to the head. The Albanians could no longer be accounted Muslims. By ten o'clock that night, not one Albanian student was left in the Medical School. No violence was done to those expelled; they were simply told that their race had forfeited all part in Turkey, that they should no longer receive Turkish Government instruction, and thrust out. Misket Hanum said she thought it hard upon the lads who were themselves quite innocent of any crime. She looked to the old poet to confirm her view of the event; but he did nothing of the kind, exclaiming with a placid smile:

## Chapter XVI: The Army of the West

"By Allah, they did well, our Turkish boys! I blame them not. Would God that everyone of that accursed race were out of Turkey!"

He then told a story of his own experiences with Albanians, which, though it smacked of bathos in the context, threw vivid light on Turkish life in Hamidian days—days which seem now remote as the crusades—so utterly has every cause of their unhappiness been swept away. You must picture the narrator as a thin-nosed, blue-eyed gentleman of seventy-three, with small thin hands, a little tremulous, crossed on the silver handle of his walking-stick, a white beard reaching almost to his waist, the fez worn low upon a noble forehead—in brief, the living image of all that is most delicate, refined, and studious in man.

"I had a garden once," he said, "a garden which I loved—almost as beautiful as yours" (he bowed to Misket Hanum). "It was at Büyükdere, on the Bosphorus. I had some beautiful old trees and many flowering and sweet-scented shrubs. I was accustomed to the place, and I could think deep thoughts there, looking from the shade across to Asia. I hoped to end my days there; I was very happy. But I was driven from it by an enemy— yes, by an enemy in time of peace—I was driven from it by Albanians."

In an evil hour, it seemed, our friend had hired two young Albanians as his gardeners. They drove away another man employed—a Turk of Anatolia —and wished him to engage a friend of theirs. They did not work well, they were lazy and insolent. At length the poet, after consultation with his friends, felt it to be his duty to dismiss them both. The rogues laughed impudently and refused to go. They then began to tease and torture him in various ways, spoiling the garden they were paid to tend. He put up with a great deal—a very great deal, he assured us—but when they took to cutting down his beautiful old trees, his pride, and using them for firewood, he felt he could endure no more.

"It is very troublesome to me to make a scene," the old man told us in his gentle voice. "I have always been a lover of tranquillity and meditation. Anger is very difficult for me. However, such impertinence and insurrection was more than I could bear. I told them I should have recourse to the police, and did so. On that they did at length depart, but with an oath of vengeance. With the assistance of some more Albanians, hired bravoes of a great man in the government, who covered all their exploits with his high protection, they laid such terror on my house that I could keep no servant. They spoilt my garden, ruined all my flowering shrubs, and made my friends afraid to come and see me without escort. They sent me word that they would kill me if I did not leave that place. Well, in the end, I sold my house and land, and emigrated to the place I now inhabit. But this new house has never seemed like home to me, though I have lived there now for twenty years and more. The disturbance to my life was too severe. I am very glad—most truly glad—that they have turned out the Albanians." The old man rubbed his hands and smiled, as he concluded.

His story sheds some light on a disputed point, for the Young Turks have been blamed for their severity towards Albanians. Albanians were the Janissaries of the Hamidian age. They openly defied the law, respecting nothing save the purse which paid them. No weak man's life or property was safe. When the revolution came, the problem of disposing of them was one of the most crucial which the Young Turks had to face. They faced it, as some say, too squarely. Not only were the bravoes banished from Constantinople, but the war was even carried into far Albania. The campaign which Javid Pasha fought in order to enforce the law for the disarming of the moutaineers was fierce and ruthless; therefore the Albanians turned on Turkey in her hour of need, betrayed Janina, murdered many Turkish officers, and starved the broken and retreating Army of the West, commanded by the

## Chapter XVI: The Army of the West

same Javid Pasha who had been their scourge, whose soldiers they reduced to eating grass—in sight of food. Albanians have great qualities, and they should make a valiant nation. It is the demand for them as mercenaries which has been their bane till now. They deserve and will maintain their independence. But, thank God, Turkey is now quit of them.

Going into town one day, my wife and I, on landing at the Bridge, got mixed up in a crowd of ragged soldiers. She clutched my arm in sudden terror and whispered in my ear; "What troops are these? I have seen nothing like these men before in Turkey." (We had gone up to the camp at Scutari the day before and she had taken snapshots of the groups of well-fed, well-dressed men, who won her heart by their delight at being photographed.) "Look at their eyes! Oh, it is horrible! Poor men! What have they seen to make them look like that?"

Ragged, unkempt, and bandaged here and there, they walked as men but half awake, and often stumbled. Their faces bore the stamp of awful suffering. The presence of a jovial and splendid Turkish officer on horseback, with a dapper sergeant in attendance, engaged in marshalling them in the roadway for their march to quarters, made their wretchedness the more apparent. But, as my wife had said, it was their eyes which made one shudder—eyes fixed and partly glazed like those of men who die in horror; or else merely mad. "It is only the Army of the West," I said, "home from Albania."

CHAPTER XVII

# THE SEASON OF THE FIRES

It was the time of fires, the hot, dry season when a spark will set alight the wooden houses of which the villages and a good part of Stamboul and Ghalata consist. Each night we heard the cry of "Yanghin Vâr!" uplifted by the watchmen as they went their rounds. The system which enables a whole region to be warned directly by the watchmen when a fire breaks out at any point is ancient, but remains efficient to the present day—efficient, that is, as concerns the speed and vigour of the warning, though I have occasionally wondered what good purpose could be served by warning a proprietor who lives, suppose, at Göztepe, that a house belonging to him was on fire at Makriköy or Therapia, at midnight when the tidings can do nothing but destroy his rest. Reformers much desire to see stone houses everywhere replace the wooden ones; but, in spite of the recurrence of disastrous fires, public opinion still remains in favour of the latter, because they are less dangerous in case of earthquake—a more dreadful, if less frequent, visitation.

Misket Hanum's house was built of stone, and she pronounced it from experience to be quite safe in the event of a great earthquake. It was a question, she assured us, merely of foundations. If the foundations were made vast and strong, the house would stand; if slight, the house would fall. But such immense foundations cost much money, and so the poor, perforce, prefer light wooden structures.

In the months of June and July 1913 the season of fires was not regarded as a normal season. The government attached unusual importance to each outbreak in the city, guarded its neighbourhood at once with troops, and worked for the extinction of the fire with more than common zeal. The confusion which arises naturally upon scenes of such disaster might, it was thought, be made the nucleus of insurrection; nor were the conspirators, many of whom still lurked in hiding, esteemed so high-souled as to be above incendiarism. I have since heard Europeans complain bitterly of the precautions taken by the commandant when fires occurred by day as a tyrannical and senseless interruption of the traffic of the city. I can only say that they were sanctioned by the situation, as I saw it from within. I well remember the excitement of our Liberal friends one afternoon, in Misket Hanum's garden, when a column of brown smoke was seen rising above the hill of gardens and kiosks which bounded our horizon towards Stamboul; and their sighs of disappointment when at evening one of our men, returning from the city, told them that the fire had been suppressed without the least disorder. They were waiting for a fire as signal of that revolution involving the extermination of the Young Turk party, for which they still kept hoping against hope.

One day in Pera, sitting after luncheon with my host, a Turk and Unionist, I heard the shout of fire and presently beheld a quaint procession pass the window at high speed. Three horse

## Chapter XVII: The Season of the Fires

fire-engines, their drivers and attendants wearing a strange barbaric form of helmet such as Chinamen once wore, were escorted on their mad career by crowds of running firemen dressed in coloured vests and shorts like gymnasts. These all had wild eyes and that stern look about the mouth which I have noticed in Egyptian watchmen when, maddened by a sense of duty, they do nothing, with tremendous fury.

"You laugh," my friend observed, "and you do right. It is an empty show. Those men, whom you have just seen passing, plunder when they get the chance. At best they only dance about among the burning buildings, brave the fire, and endeavour to show off their daring in the public eye. They get in the way of the real workers, who are generally soldiers. A vast amount of force and energy thus runs to waste among us every day. This elaborate fire-system, though efficient as a drill or exercise, has never by misfortune been directed at the actual fire."

Tapping on the window, he then beckoned a policeman who was passing by. The man ran up, saluting.

"Where is the fire?" my friend inquired.

"Low down between the bridges, bey efendim!"

"Is it a big one?"

"Likely, bey efendim!"

A few minutes later, when we took a carriage to go over to Stamboul, our driver told us that a strong cordon of troops prevented our going by the straight road to the Bridge.

"On account of the fire?" my friend questioned.

"Who knows, bey efendim!" was the answer, as the man whipped up his wretched horses. Although the war, as we then thought, was ended, none of the decent horses commandeered for it had yet come back into the city streets. The conjunction of bad beasts with hilly roads produced some cruel lashing, which, when seen by tourists, breeds a prejudice against the Turks, although the hackney coachmen, at any rate upon the Pera side, are mostly Christians. In our own village where the arabajis were Muslims I saw no cruelty. In the same way I have heard people in England say they hated Turks because of the way the said Turks leered at women in the Earl's Court Exhibitions, when to my certain knowledge the objectionable persons—gimcrack stall-holders—were Syrian Christians to a man. Everyone who wears a fez being a Turk to the uninitiated, I may perhaps be pardoned this digression to point out that Ottoman Christians also wear the fez, and in one point at least have earned the Turks a bad name undeservedly. The Turks are generally very kind to animals. The straight road to the Bridge being thus barred, our carriage was obliged to go a long way round; and even then, when not far from the point desired, was stopped by soldiers in a narrow street, and ordered to go back. To turn the horses there was quite impossible; their backing was a ticklish and nerve-racking process; however, we at length emerged. The driver tried another turning. We were stopped again. This time we alighted and dismissed the carriage. My friend, who was a man in some authority, well-known by sight to every Muslim in the city, essayed to pass the group of soldiers who had stopped us. They spread out instantly and barred the way, with—

"Yassak (It is forbidden), bey efendim!"

He endeavoured to remonstrate with them, pointing out that it was not in our intentions to go near the fire, whose whereabouts could be located by a cloud of smoke a good way off. Still,

"Yassak, bey efendim!" was the answer.

I ventured to suggest to my companion that a five-piaster piece might overcome the difficulty. He laughed at that, amid his irritation.

"Dear friend," he said, "we are not dealing now with the tulúmbajis (the running firemen), and all the rubbish which they typify—the picturesque corrupt old pageant of administration. We are confronted now by Jemâl Bey and discipline, by something living, stern and capable, which will, please God, in time absorb the other. These soldiers know me

## Chapter XVII: The Season of the Fires

and my influence. Be sure, if they refuse us passage, knowing me, they would not grant it for a Turkish pound apiece. These are the wrong kind of men to offer bribes to. Try the small officials and the doorkeepers of public buildings."

We then amused ourselves by circumambulating the cordon, which was complete and strong, isolating a whole quarter of the town. Had the outbreak been the work of revolutionaries they could hardly have escaped, and no reinforcements short of a trained army could have come to them. Considering the rapidity with which the operation had been carried out—for the troops, we heard, were there before the firemen—and the evident devotion of the men employed, I shared my friend's enthusiasm when he murmured "Jemâl Bey's a man!"

But the interruption of all business in a business quarter was naturally not appreciated by the men of business who, when there was no insurrection after all, proclaimed it senseless. The Turks, we will agree, are most unbusinesslike; their commercial instincts are comparatively undeveloped; they still pay reverence to soldiers, poets and the learned rather than financiers, and prize the honour of their nation above gold. Yet it cannot be denied that they possess a gift for management, and are at present making giant strides towards that "efficiency" which Europeans generally deem the highest good. They have accepted once for all the point of view of Europe, and are using every effort to live up to it. All that they ask is leave to work out their own problems, and advance to modern progress in the way they understand. Europeans, judging them by Europe's smartest standard, find them wanting. But any man who thinks of Asia must, I think, applaud them. Turkey is the present head of a progressive movement extending throughout Asia and North Africa. She is also the one hope of the Islamic world. That she should be encouraged to advance in independence on the soil of Europe, bringing up the East, seems more desirable, politically, than that Europe should cut up and then exploit the Turkish Empire. The Pera attitude is roughly this: the world is for the Europeans (which to the mind of Eastern Christians means the Christians); no one else has any right to profit or consideration. It cannot surely be the attitude of British statesmen who are called upon to rule an Eastern empire. The progress which the Turks are making is genuine and rapid, for a close observer. In this of the fires—a small particular—it may be noticed. In the summer of 1913, outbreaks were extinguished much more promptly than had ever been the case before, thanks to the soldiers; and the project of a new fire-brigade is being mooted, to be run on military, not gymnastic, lines.

When we walked round the cordon at three o'clock that afternoon, a considerable fire was raging, sending up dense clouds of smoke. An hour and a half later when from the deck of a steamer I looked out for it, it was extinguished; no smoke was rising from the mass of picturesque old houses by the waterside.

## CHAPTER XVIII
# OTTOMAN EDUCATION

My friend Mehmet was presented by his parents with a pet "lamb"—which seemed to me a full-grown sheep—an object of solicitude to all the household and especially the gardeners, who would run and extricate it gently with a flow of tender words when, at sight of strangers like myself, it ran in sudden panic round the tree where it was tethered and got hopelessly entangled in its rope. About the same time similar pet lambs appeared in many other of our neighbour's houses. The cause of the phenomenon was in the Muslim calendar. We had arrived at just that interval from a great feast required for the right fattening of lamb. The fact that they would ultimately have to eat their darlings was kept hidden from the children, or, if known to them, appeared as dim and distant as old age. One saw family groups, the father leading a pet sheep, the children fondling it or clutching at its wool, upon the steamers on the Bosphorus and at the railway stations, where, before the booking-office, there is an affair of barriers intended to control the crowd when buying tickets. The poorer Turks and all the native Christians, men and women, however long a time they have to spare, are invariably panic-stricken at the sight of persons buying tickets, and rush madly for the wicket, quite regardless of each other's welfare. In the midst of such a scrimmage at the terminus I once saw an unfortunate pet sheep appertaining to a man who had just bought his ticket and was trying to get out. His children with him kicked and fought at the surrounding legs, protecting their beloved, which escaped at last, uninjured.

Sheep being thus associated in my mind with families, it was with amazement that I saw one in possession of a bachelor, a young man from a distant province of the Empire, who, I knew, had no relations in Constantinople. It was in the long shed on the floating stage below the Bridge, the waiting-room for those who fare towards Haïdar Pasha. Having just come in out of the blinding sunlight I could not trust my eyes at first. At the far end of the shanty stood a figure in the neat dark uniform of the Military School, the crescent shining on its kalpak of black astrakhan—a figure stationary under difficulties in its struggle with a good-sized sheep which for ever made short rushes to escape but was restrained by force. It seemed familiar. I stared, and then drew nearer, staring still. A military salute, with cordial blessings in good Arabic, finally dispelled all doubt. Returning the salute in the civilian manner, I took a seat upon a packing case hard by the struggler, and complimented him, with reservations as against the evil eye, upon the health and beauty of his pet.

"Amân!" (Mercy!) he exclaimed. "It is not mine. Use no precautions! Curse it outright, if you desire to do so, for, Allah be my witness, I detest it. I was asked to hold it by a fellow-traveller, who said that he would not be gone a minute; and here have I been hanging on to it for two whole hours!"

He had no knowledge of the owner of the sheep —a kind of peasant—had never seen him in this world before. The man

## Chapter XVIII: Ottoman Education

had come up just like that, with "Jânum (My soul), for the love of Allah, ease me of this lamb a minute." Besought thus, "for the love of Allah," he could not refuse; although he thought that people used the name of God too lightly. I suggested that he should pass his trouble on to someone else good-natured in the same way that it had been foisted on to him. But "No," was his reply, "I promised that I would hold the animal until he came again, so I must do so."

I left him holding on to the pet lamb, which was not his, still struggling, when I ran on board the steamer, warned by a hoot that it was going to start. My parting words were: "May our Lord relieve thee speedily!"

He was relieved a half hour later, as I heard from him at our next meeting, when he manifested not the least resentment of the incident, and yet would not consent to treat it as a joke as I did. He chose rather to regard it as symbolic of the need of all the Empire for a course of training in responsibility. The owner of the sheep was poor and quite illiterate; he did not recognize the worth of time nor yet the call for strict adherence to a word once uttered; whereas he himself (my Arab friend), having been educated in the government schools and being an officer of sorts inured to discipline, had learnt the great importance of these things. Therefore he kept his word religiously, acknowledging a duty towards the poor man, his tormentor, as representative of all the backward and misguided persons in the realm. It was a duty of forbearance and of education. He had discharged it, first by holding on to that confounded sheep for close upon three hours, and secondly by reading the delinquent, when he did at last return, a lesson which he would remember to his dying day. All this he told me with the eagerness of an apostle. The incident was nothing banal nor annoying in his memory, since he could attach it to the great ideal of uplifting patriotism which warms the blood and fires the brain of every scion of the revolution.

During the six months I spent in Turkey it was my good

fortune to know many of these children of the new regime, or my outlook on the future of that country and of Islam would not have been so hopeful as it is. Strict Muslims without superstition, they are growing up in love with duty, proud of their burden of responsibility, devoted to their country beyond words, tolerant of all beliefs which do not savour of sedition, thoughtful, self-reliant, trustworthy. They are perhaps a shade pedantic, a thought too serious in their opinions to attract the stranger, but that is but the outcome of the times they live in, by no means times of gaiety for Turkish patriots. No Turk, perhaps in the same circumstances, would have been so literal and so punctilious as was my Arab friend in dealing with so small a problem; the difference of mentality between the races always struck me; but a Turk of the same age and education would have held the same opinions with the same enthusiasm, the same resolve to practise what he preached.

When I hear English people talking of the Turks as hopeless, with no vitality left in them, no enthusiasm and no prospects, I can only think that they have never met with the young men of Turkey, or have met with those only who have been educated among Europeans. In this opinion I am hardened by the fact that all the Ottoman young men—whether Christian or Muslim— of my acquaintance informed me that I was the first European with whom they had ever held much conversation; whereas the other type of youth inclines to seek out Europeans, and adopt their cynical and hopeless standpoint towards the Muslim world. The old Muslim education, medieval and religious, has ceased to meet the needs of the community. The new Muslim education has but just begun, but already it is running through the land like wildfire reviving the innumerable old foundations, bringing new ones into life. In the interval, the Turk and Arab, brought in contact with the ways of Europe, has had to supplement his Muslim education by a sojourn at some mission school, where his faith in Islam was undermined without impairing his contempt for Christianity; he was imbued with the commercial faith of Europe which derides true patriotism, at any rate as understood by Turks; and in many cases won to lifelong admiration of some foreign power, whose servant he became in the intrigues of after life. Thus Kiamil Pasha was the friend of England; another Pasha was the friend of France or Germany; no one was especially the friend of Turkey. Turkey did not appear to them as a beloved country, but as a position which could only be maintained by the favour of this or that great Power of Europe. There was excuse for the secession of these individuals from the Ottoman nation—their "cosmopolitanism," as they would have called it proudly—in the old days when Turkey groaned beneath a cruel despotism. The nation then had really no existence. Today the land is free and bent on progress; and I find no excuse for their continued scorn of it.

For see what has been done in these five years since the Constitution was proclaimed—five years of ceaseless trouble from without. The tyrant's spies, the rich men's bravoes have been swept away; slavery has been abolished; brigandage has been put down. Sane endeavour has replaced the old corruption born of fatalism. The army has been fed and clothed with the result that the disorders which disgraced the wretched soldiers in old days have disappeared. European women, in their dress which still seems shameful to old-fashioned Turks, can now walk in the markets of Stamboul without fear of being pinched or hustled as in Pera. Dark corners of administration have been brought to light, and fanaticism, having no longer any place in which to hide, is gone, has given way to an enlightened patriotism. The Turkish Post-Office and other branches of administration, once deplorable, now may be compared for their efficiency with the same departments in the government of European countries. Turks can now speak and write their thoughts without the fear of murder or imprisonment. They can travel from Constantinople to İzmit without a special permit from the government. In all directions there has been improvement and reform. All in five years! And yet the Pera people will inform you, nothing has been done. It may be that they reckon this as nothing when compared with the vast work which still remains to do. But I think the explanation of their attitude is rather that they never think about the Turks at all, nor care for the condition of the country save as it affects themselves.

## CHAPTER XIX
## COSMOPOLITAN EDUCATION

I was Standing leaning on the rail beside the hut where they sell tickets for the Kadıköy steamer, watching the moving swarm of little boats between the floating platform and the quay, so dense that one could see the water only momentarily as a flash or sparkle here and there amid the throng, when someone coming up behind me said in Arabic:

"How is your health, O sage? What tidings from Arabistan?"

It was a young clerk in one of the Ministries whom I knew slightly. He spoke French well and Arabic abominably, but after a conversation in the train one evening when I had maintained that Turks ought to learn Arabic rather than French, he always, when he met me subsequently, aired his store of Arabic (lapsing gradually into Turkish, which was by that time familiar to me) pretending to have been convinced by my remarks on that occasion. He asked if I was going to the boat, and learning that to be the case, called my attention to the fact that it had just come in. We might as well, he thought, repair on board and choose our seats before the crowd arrived. On all previous occasions of our meeting I had been attracted by his jovial, reckless air; but today he appeared careworn and exceedingly depressed. His conversation too was all despair. When I remarked that things were looking better for the Turks, he answered with a shrug:

"What does it matter? We are finished! To give us hope is only to prolong our agony. Now here am I! You see me! I have had the best of educations. I speak French and German fluently. I am as intelligent, I dare to think, as any Frank on earth; but it is all useless. I am young, and should, they say, be hopeful; but what hope exists for me? We are all like that—aimless, undirected, unable to apply our knowledge to the work of life. We are inconsequent, uncertain in our actions, having no ideal."

From these remarks I judged my friend to be a Liberal, for since the failure of their great attempt at revolution they all upon-occasion talked like that. Besides, the characteristics which he claimed for the whole Turkish people were not those of the Unionists of my acquaintance.

"What is it that is wrong with us?" he asked rhetorically. And when I interrupted with: "I think it is that you are trying to be something which you can never be, something which nobody with any sense would wish to be—a European," he answered:

"No, it is not that, O sage! The reason is the dreadful lives we live at home, in private. If you knew our Turkish women—their ignorance, their pride, their narrow minds!"

As it happened I did know about a score of them, and had heard, I think it probable, more talk of them than he had. I knew them to be generally charming, trained to submission yet high-spirited, and far less narrow-minded than the women of the West. But I did not interrupt him by an observation.

"If we enjoyed as you do," he continued, "the companionship of wives of high intelligence, well-educated, tactful, capable of understanding us and participating in our intellectual cares and interests, we might be men. As it is, what are we? Less than nothing! We go to school, we learn all that there is to know, we work in our employment: of what profit is it? The home life, I assure you, ruins all. With our women there is no pretence at understanding possible. They have no civilization and no delicacy. We shall never become men till that is altered. And how to alter it, I ask you, with such women as ours, so obstinate and so fanatical?"

He spoke with evident emotion, and I even fancied at one moment that I saw the teardrop in his eye. As the boat began to fill up with the evening crowd of government employés returning to their country houses, he was hailed on all hands. Usually the most hilarious of jolly companions, this evening he appeared morose, and, after formal salutations, entrenched himself behind his newspaper and spoke no more. I did the same till we were in the middle of the Bosphorus, when I looked out as usual for the "wind-chasers" or "souls of the damned," little sea-birds ever flying up towards Beykos, skimming the sapphire water in an endless train. I saw that my neighbour, the despondent Torghut Bey, was also watching them. Was he thinking of the legend which would make those birds the erring souls of all the fair ones who have been thrown into those waters for their naughtiness; and was he wishing that the pretty Turkish ladies of today might all be drowned in sacks immediately, and English suffragists imported to replace them?

At Haïdar Pasha, as I climbed the broad white steps to the railway station, he was once more beside me in the crowd, talking as if there had been no break in our conversation.

"And our religion! How benighted, how behind the times it is! It hampers us on all occasions when we seek improvement. We need a Luther badly. The whole system of our law is antiquated and obstructive. Our government is childish and the scorn of Europe. You are good enough to champion us, O sage, but we are rotten to the core, degraded, finished!"

My saying with a laugh that it was just the same with England in the opinion of a good number of my fellow-countrymen made him more gloomy and, I think, prevented him from sitting with me in the train as he had first intended. At all events he let me enter the first coach alone, where, chancing on some men I knew, I quite forgot poor Torghut Bey and his despair until, arrived in Misket Hanum's garden, I was greeted by a group of Turkish friends with the inquiry:

"Well, what adventures have you had today?"

No one waited for an answer to the question, which was a mere gibe at my habit of exalting common incidents. The ladies went on with their conversation instantly, while one of the men in company drew near to me. To him I mentioned my despondent friend, his deep disgust with Turkish women and consequent despair of the whole country.

My hearer laughed:

"He must be in some scrape. I take it that home life, the cares of matrimony and the rest of it, amount to much the same in every country of the world. Some are unlucky, and they blame the system, while others, being happy, think it good. Go to Paris or Pekin, and I imagine that you would find the same divergence of opinions in very much the same proportion that you find it here."

He called his wife out from the knot of ladies, inquiring: "Do you know if Torghut Bey has had a quarrel with his wife or her relations lately?"

"Which Torghut?" was of course the answer. The identity of my Torghut having been established in her understanding, she seemed to think likely that there had been trouble; but said no more than that the wife of the Torghut in question was of her acquaintance, a girl extremely well-brought-up and educated, but a little proud; as was but natural, for she came of a very good family. Her husband asked her to find out if there had been a quarrel lately; and, when I protested that she must not go to trouble on my account, asked if I had lived to my age in the world without perceiving that a woman's dearest joy was in researches into other women's business. He assured me that the charming lady there beside us, for guileless that she looked, carried in her head the secret history of every Turkish family of any standing, and was always on the watch to add a chapter. The lady, who kept smiling enigmatically, bade me never to believe a word he said, and pointed out, with perfect justice of retort, that occasionally men's curiosity urged women on to such research as in the present case. She asked to know the reason of our curiosity. The substance of the young man's talk with me was then reported by her husband; whereupon she told us all we wished to know, having merely held the story in reserve till she had drawn out ours. After hearing from her that poor Torghut's wife was proud, I had imagined that he might have serious reason to be discontented, judging from the matrimonial experience of other Turks of my acquaintance with young ladies "of a very good family." One friend, a youthful pasha of the old régime, had been married willy nilly by the daughter of a Grand Vizier, who made life hateful to him by her airs and jealousies, treating him like a servant in her house. His feelings towards her, naturally, grew vindictive; and when the Revolution came and her relations lost their power to ruin him, he soon divorced her. Some months after the divorce a bundle came for him by runner. It contained a new-born baby and a sheet of paper with the words:

"This is yours. Thank God, I am now quit of you." If Torghut had espoused a tigress of that breed, I should have pitied him and understood his desperation. But his case, it appeared, was very different.

"A pretty youth to sit in judgment on our morals!" said the lady, our enlightener, in tones of rich amusement. "His wife is evidently much too good for him, but then it was a love-match, so she has herself to blame. Some time ago she found out that he was a gambler. He used to lie to her, pretending that it was his business at the Ministry which made him late at nights, when all the while he was frequenting the low haunts of Pera. She scolded him; he promised to amend. Two nights ago he never came at all. She made inquiries in the morning—sent to Stamboul—to his Ministry—went herself into the town to seek for tidings, but had no word of him until last evening, when he came home in a pitiable state. She was very angry, naturally, and ashamed for him. She threatened to sue for a divorce, but in the end forgave him. No doubt the being rated by a woman preyed upon his manly dignity, and that is why he spoke to you so feelingly against us women and the state of Turkey. A dissolute, absurd young man, who has never thought on any serious subject! Judge of the value of his views on our poor country!"

Some Europeans in Constantinople may be heard declaring that the Turks themselves despair of Turkey, and admit that they are finished, being quite degenerate. To all such theorists I would commend the story of poor Torghut Bey.

## CHAPTER XX
## CHECKS ON PROGRESS

The word "love-match" as applied in the foregoing chapter to a Turkish marriage may strike the English reader with astonishment. I have already mentioned how, among advanced, French-educated Turks, the circle of a woman's male acquaintance has been enlarged beyond the bounds of kindred and affinity. That being so, it follows that a Turkish maiden of today can sometimes make a marriage of affection without transgressing either decency or etiquette. In my own circle I was witness of a courtship, which differed little from an English wooing, between young people well acquainted with each other. At their wedding the ceremony of the "Koltuk" and unveiling had, naturally, no significance. They went through it, laughing; and repeated it, when conversation languished, as a joke. Their marriage feast, as Misket Hanum put it, was "Ghayet alafranga" (in the extreme Prankish manner), and on the morrow bride and bridegroom started for the Riviera on their honeymoon.

One of my friends, a man by no means of the modern school, allowed his daughter to contract a marriage with a youth of her own choosing, whom she had met in circumstances he did not approve. That sort of marriage had, he told me, one advantage for a parent in that the girl could never blame him if it turned out badly; whereas in the old-fashioned marriage by arrangement, she, if unhappy, made incessant claims upon his purse and influence. Girls of a certain education nowadays were making it a point of honour not to marry men they did not know, and where they had no money or exceptional attractions were, of course, left waiting. In his opinion, founded on the observation of a lifetime, marriage as the result of youthful passion seldom led to happiness.

Even the closely guarded Turkish maiden will generally manage to obtain a glimpse of her betrothed before the wedding; more rarely will contrive a meeting and a talk with him. In the first case, she arranges through some female go-between that the man shall walk in a certain spot, where she can see him from her lattice, at a certain hour, wearing a flower or favour she has sent to him. In the second, the place of meeting would in general be some cemetery, regarded as a kind of sanctuary where a lady, being veiled, can wander without other escort than a friend or woman servant. No more romantic trysting-place could be imagined than, for instance, the great cemetery of Scutari—a forest of old cypress-trees, such deep shade that every object appears strange, mysterious, remote from life as is the bottom of the sea. The narrow headstones, taller than a man, incline this way and that, with the disorder of a natural undergrowth. Here and there a grander mausoleum, a cubic structure with a dome, rises to half the height of the gnarled tree-trunks; here and there are full-robed figures flitting silently, or seated in a group around some grave. The mystic grove—for so it really seems—its graven headstones like the runic signs of lost antiquity— extends for miles, and could conceal a thousand lovers; while its gloom and weirdness impart just the atmosphere which Turkish lovers value most in love. But the maiden who will venture so far is a rarity. Most girls inspect their bridegrooms from a guarded distance.

Misket Hanum once amused us with a full description of the way in which princesses choose their man. A number of photographs of young men of station are submitted to the lady, who, lounging on a sofa, takes them one by one, studies and talks them over with her women. Perhaps she sends them all away as unattractive or too low of stature—for every Turkish damsel in her teens adores tall men and means to wed a giant— and sends for a fresh batch. When one attracts her, she proclaims the fact, and orders the original to be produced, and made to walk before her lattice, then to ride on horseback, then to run or jump. If she disapproves of him in any posture, she rejects him and demands another. Sometimes the chosen is not in the list submitted, but someone she has seen by chance from her carriage or caïque. In one case that I know of he was married, and the father of two children; but the princess still declared that she must have him. He must merely keep his other wife and children in the background; he could go and see them sometimes. The man, though much embarrassed, had to do her will, and in the sequel, as I know, was very happy, the princess being charming to his children and the other wife.

To those who see in the French manners of some Turks the birth of a new social order in Islam, many of the old religious rules and ordinances seem anachronisms. There is desire for their reform in "advanced" circles. Poor Torghut's cry: "We need a Luther!" has been uttered in my hearing by more serious thinkers. It is clearly no advantage to the Turks as Muslims that their prayers and all religious offices should be in Arabic. This absurdity—for such it would have seemed to the Apostle of Islam, the greatest protestant that ever lived— has led to the appointment of a special order of proficients, like a priesthood—the thing the Prophet most abhorred on earth. Nothing of the sort exists in Arab countries. There is no religious reason why a large proportion of the prayers should not be said in Turkish, or why the khôja of today should not return to his true Muslim status as a simple "person learned in religion"—no reason whatsoever, save expediency. The demand for such reform is still so far from general that the great majority of Turks could be relied on furiously to oppose the slightest change.

Occasionally I have heard progressive Turks speak of the khôjas in a body as a bar to progress. During my stay in Turkey I conversed with many khôjas, having a love for the Muslim religion and the character of its professed students, and I cannot say that I should call them that. None of the various opinions that I heard expressed by them could, by any judgment, be pronounced reactionary. They all looked forward, for example, to the relative emancipation of women upon Islamic lines analogous to those already followed with success by certain of the Russian Muslims. The better education of women they one and all regarded as among the country's greatest needs. If one may take it that the little fads and prejudices of the English clergy are compatible with toleration, then none of them was in the least intolerant. With the exception of a few political thinkers, they were the only persons whom I met who seemed to me to sit in judgment upon new ideas, rejecting what was manifestly evil or absurd. They were far from being, I should say, opposed to progress unless it were to progress of a hurried ill-considered kind. They urged the need of circumspection and much patience.

"But patience requires time, and time is not allowed us," a Unionist said once upon my talking in this strain. "The European menace is immediate. The moment their 'sick man' gave signs of a return to health the doctors, turned to butchers, swore to make an end of him. They are only waiting for agreement and a good excuse. Thus threatened, have we

## Chapter XX: Checks on Progress

any time to think? Must we not grasp the best plan that occurs to us and force it forward against all opponents?"

In truth, for me, a European, to talk to Turks, thus threatened by all Europe, of patience and deliberation, was ridiculous. All the same the khôjas are quite right in their contention. To offend one ignorant religious prejudice at this juncture, to proceed too fast though in the right direction, might be to rob the people of their stomach for the coming fight.

"If you knew with what resentment the ambassadors of certain Powers oppose us every time we aim at serious reform, you would have no doubt of the hostility of their intentions," my friend added.

I had no doubt of that hostility, which seems to be accepted, outside Turkey, as intrinsic to the situation of that ill-starred country; is even pleaded by the diplomatically minded in excuse for their withholding sympathy from Turkey in her strife for progress. It would be to waste that sympathy, they argue, Turkey being doomed by secret sentence of the Powers. They turn their sympathy in some direction where they see a fair chance of its meeting with material reward. Such views are common in the vulgar sphere of politics, but in the realm of letters they can claim no standing. Here it is still lawful to applaud the fighting hero, to uphold the cause of justice, though unpopular. Here we may speak the truth against diplomacy:— The state of Turkey is more full of hope today than ever in that country's former history, more full of hope than is the state of any European country. Its hopelessness, of which we hear so much, is in the greedy eyes of Europe, nowhere else.

Islam has been so widely and sententiously misrepresented, even by a section of its own adherents, that I feel that I am courting laughter when I state: (1) that it is no less tolerant than Christianity, (2) that it is not a foe to human progress.

On my first contention ponderous tomes by learned Christian writers as well as texts from the Coran can be produced against me. But if the Coran is carefully perused from end to end, and its various texts on this subject carefully collated, the pros and cons for toleration—at any rate of Jews and Christians—will be found to balance. In like manner the pronouncements (fatwas) of Shaykh-ul-Islam and learned judges will be found now leaning towards the widest tolerance, now wearing the dark colour of extreme fanaticism, according (and this is the crux of the whole question) as Christendom attacked the Muslims or kept peace with them. A learned Shaykh explained the matter thus to me:

"A Christian who loves Muslims and respects their faith must be counted as a Muslim by all true believers everywhere. He is in the way with us, bound on the same journey, and to hold aloof from him or flout him would be sin." And he proceeded to declaim two texts of Scripture, one to the effect that such a Christian shall be welcome to take part in Muslim worship, the other this:

"God is our Lord, and your Lord, unto us our works and unto you your works. No quarrel between us and you, for God will gather us both in, and unto Him we shall return."

I could quote many instances to show that the significance of these words has never been lost sight of by good Muslims, whereas the Gospel texts "Other sheep I have which are not of this fold," "He that is not against us is for us," and so forth (making as they do for toleration) have been overlooked by Christians. The Christian who avowedly hates Muslims, or assails them, is naturally to be treated as an enemy. Thus it will be seen that Muslim intolerance of Christianity, as well in theory as in practice, is in response and in direct proportion to the Christian's hatred of Islam. Few will, I think, deny that the religion of the Muslim is more enlightened and progressive in the abstract, than that of the majority of Eastern Christians; which brings me to the second point of my contending: that Islam is not a foe to human progress.

## CHAPTER XXI
# ISLAM AND PROGRESS

The Muslim religion has been blamed for traits of character which are found in all the native inhabitants of warm climates. If the Christians in the hotter Muslim countries do today excel Muslims in energy it is owing to a difference of race and not of creed; but, personally, I believe the Christian's lead in this respect to be unreal, a mere affair of bustle and vivacity. The Muslim's energies have up to now been spent perforce on war and the routine of agriculture; whereas the efforts of the Christian, who, until the Revolution, was exempt from military service, have been turned to commerce and the peaceful arts of self-advancement. The Muslim has for years known little peace, although he long ago gave up aggression. It must also be remembered that the Muslims of the Turkish Empire have been much neglected, the attention of the Government being absorbed in efforts to ward off encroachments of the Powers of Europe; while the Christian population has been nursed by missionaries and protected by the envoys of those Powers. Taking all these facts into account and also the tremendous increase of energy and initiative noticeable in the Turkish people since the Revolution, I believe that the Muslim population, given peace and a fair government, will prove, if not superior to the Christian in commercial enterprise, superior in every kind of honest work. The Turks, as a white race, have a natural precedence over the many-coloured races of the Muslim world. They are Hanafis, members of the only Sunnite sect of Islam which accepts man's reason as a guide before tradition; whereas the Egyptians, for example, are mostly Shafi'is and hold the opposite opinion —by temperament, it is certain, rather than free choice. That the Turks are capable of understanding Europe more than are any other race of Muslims is deserving of remembrance. The whole Muslim East is rising, and will go on rising more fiercely under Christian than under Muslim rule. If progressive Turkey must be crushed, as Europe says, then one day Europe will behold an Arab Empire, with little of the toleration and good temper of the Turk. Much as I love the Arabs and respect their many virtues, I recognise a difference in their mentality, which makes it most desirable, from Europe's standpoint, that the Turks should long remain the leaders of the Muslim world. Alas, there is no head to Europe, only limbs and bell; so to what or whom can one appeal?

Much has been made of the common sayings, "Kismet dir" (It is fate), "Kismetim dir" (It is my lot in life), and so on, to demonstrate the fatalism of the Turk. This fatalism is ascribed to his religion rather hastily. That everybody's fate is preordained of God the Muslim certainly believes; well, so do many Christians. But, as the whole world is the material of each man's fate, the predestined course of which cannot be known by any till the Day of Judgment, this belief would seem to preclude energetic action and initiative no more than does the Christian doctrine of self-sacrifice. There is, I know, a text in the Coran:

"The fate of each is tied about his neck, and no-one laden may bear another's load," which has been taken by some critics to imply the opposite of, "Bear ye one another's burdens." In its context it does nothing of the kind, referring evidently to a man's relation to his works at the Last Judgment; while passages which preach the brotherhood of all believers, the need of charity and mutual help, abound in the Coran. In fact, as I have said already here and there, the failings generally charged to Islam, are either incidental to the climate in which Muslims live, or else, and I believe more truly, the result of long subjection to a despotism, which discouraged all endeavour of a peaceful kind. The genuine Turks are not a lazy race, as witness the amount of corn exported every year from Haïdar Pasha, the produce of those provinces of Anatolia of which the rural population is almost entirely Turkish. The Turkish peasant is exceedingly industrious, and has gone on working doggedly under conditions which would have broken the heart of any other agriculturist. But the slightest deviation or excursion from the mere routine of work, the least display of enterprise on his part, was punished by increased taxation; and so, routine being his sole refuge of philosophy, he clung to it with "Kismet" and due praise to Allah. Now at last he is emancipated, he has leave to be a man the arena of his fate which man had narrowed, is now once more made worldwide as it came from God. In this the Turks behold the restoration of Islâm.

The work is but begun. The greatest task of the reformers, next to the reorganisation of the public schools, is the revival of the local governments, through which alone the poorer Muslims can be quickly raised to the position of responsible, free citizens, the rich compelled to help them and themselves. The road which ran past Misket Hanum's garden gate, beneath an avenue of fine acacias, was full of mounds and deep depressions, being quite unmade. It was the sole way of approach to thirty kiosks, inhabited by people of large means, who had all been grumbling over the state of the road, complaining of the Government, for more than twenty years. When I suggested that they should take the work in hand themselves and do it properly, they looked aghast and said that it was not their business. It is true that in the days of Abdul Hamid they could not have done it, for their action would have made a noise, and might have been resented as a personal affront by some high functionary, whose titular concern was roads. But now, when the Government is anxious for improvement, and, having more than it can do, would welcome help, their horror at the thought was purely ludicrous in men who talked so much of progress and the value of initiative.

Again, it is the custom of the householder to take all rubbish to his boundary wall and cast it forth on to some road or public footpath. Rich men, who keep a lot of gardeners, observe this custom. While their gardens are kept beautifully neat within, the outer wall is an offence to passers-by. Responsibility ends there. The rubbish stinks; the owner of the garden, walking in his fair domain, curses the Government for allowing such a nuisance to remain where he can smell it. "In civilised countries," he remarks, "they send men daily to remove all refuse." In our road, Misket Hanum was, I think, the only householder who ever made her men go out beyond her garden gate with brooms or shovels, who ever had a bad hole in the road filled up, or proposed co-operation of the neighbours for the road's improvement.

When I laid examples such as these before my Unionist adviser, he cried out in some impatience: "They concern rich people. We have no hope in the rich; we know them, they are useless. But the poor are very different. Among them you will find both energy and public spirit— undeveloped, it is true, as yet, but evident." I had also some friends among the poor, and I agreed with him as to their vigour and their greater possibilities, while not despairing of the rich as he did. The rich, though still dejected by the fall of Abdul Hamid, would prove of service, I felt sure, when once the new regime appealed to them, as it could only do by a revival of the local governments, through which the poor would also gain the stimulus they needed, a sense of being something in the scheme of things. At present the poor Muslims still retain the feeling that outside the circle of their own immediate friends, outside their village, there is constant trickery and fear of foul oppression. The train will very likely start an hour too soon, the steamer has a stupid purpose to go off without them, their fellow-men are minded to frustrate their every aim. Their notions of the outer world are vaguely hostile, as the result of past experience of injustice, from which a man's own weight or nimbleness alone could save him. My wife was terrified one day at Haïdar Pasha by the rush of the crowd to get on board the steamer for Stamboul. Foolishly she turned round to remonstrate halfway up the gangway, and was very nearly pushed into the water by an enormous sort of mattress advancing on a porter's legs. The bearer of the mattress, seeing nothing but his feet, marched straight ahead, impersonal as Juggernaut. When we recounted the adventure afterwards at Misket Hanum's, a Turkish lady present murmured gravely:

"I congratulate you upon your escape, Madame; for had you fallen in the water, it is highly probable that no one would have moved a hand to save you."

She told a story of her personal knowledge of three women being drowned within reach of a crowd of boats and boatmen. I replied with one of mine, about a Syrian Arab who was walking in the country with a friend of his, when that friend stepped abruptly into a disused well or cistern such as is often met with in the country round Jerusalem. The Arab never thought of running to bring help, never paused to ascertain whether his friend yet lived, never even seemed to feel a thrill of horror; but simply raised his eyes to Heaven with the funeral oration: "La hawla wa la qûwwata illa bi'llahi 'l'aliyyil 'l'azim" (There is no power nor might save in God the High, the Tremendous), and tranquilly proceeded on his way. Yet I knew him for an excellent, kind-hearted man. It was only that he was resigned to anything which might befall in this strange world. "In the midst of life we are in death" was his sole comment when he told of the occurrence. He accepted facts as they appeared to him, unchangeable, coming as he thought directly from the hand of God.

The Turkish lady laughed at my anecdote, but said: "The Turks are different. Our people are not quite so apathetic as your Arab. They have been discouraged in the past from rescue of the drowning by dread of interfering in some great man's game. Stories of misfortune consequent upon such rescue are still told among them. Their indifference, I think, is but a legacy of old unhappy days. And let me tell you that the boatmen who looked on while the three girls of whom I spoke were drowning near the landing-stage were most of them not Turks at all, but Christians."

She told us then of gallant rescues done by Turks. One man, an officer, happened to be on board a steamboat leaving Pasha Baghcheh on the Bosphorus, when a man fell overboard. The officer unslung his sword upon the instant, and was in the act of tearing off his tunic when his servant sprang on him and bellowed for assistance, supposing his poor master had gone mad. The officer called him a fool and flung him off, bidding him make the captain stop the boat. At once, with the command which carried explanation with it, the soldier from a hindrance became serviceable. He caused the steamer to put back, and was standing ready with a rope to help his master when the latter with his burden swam in reach.

I have picked this story out from others, many of them more dramatic, because it seems to me to be a parable of subject Turkey, so long subject that it does not yet know how to move in freedom. At present it still gapes upon the strange procession of events not understanding. Admit the poor Turks to the secret, teach them the sense of what is going on; above all, give them each some definite small work to do, and they will show an energy, a handiness, and a devotion to amaze the critic who had judged them in their frozen state.

The prejudice against the Muslim is, I know, deep-rooted in the Christian mind. But let the reader ask himself, after a glance at the ideals, the hopes, and eke the difficulties of progressive Turkey whether such a people, though Muslim, does not deserve the toleration of the civilised. It is Turkey's exclusion from that magic circle which includes such shining lights as Russia and the Balkan States, her not being "Christian," simply, which is held to justify her persecution, and all kinds of brigandage at her expense. It will no doubt be held to justify the partition of her Asiatic territory (already, as I hear, arranged for by the Powers) and will give the character of a crusade to yet another cruel massacre.

The deity behind the Powers of Europe being, as it is, not God but Mammon, one must protest at least against the dragging in of Christianity as a mere blind to the true nature of the deed in contemplation. This is nothing but a crime against humanity. Such crimes in history never lack their Nemesis.

## CHAPTER XXII
# FAREWELLS

One morning in July I left our village by the morning train which government officials usually took to go to town, and, chancing on a friend and neighbour, talked to him incessantly until we parted at the Bridge. As a rule we disagreed profoundly, and were ready to abuse each other in a cordial way, but that morning he endorsed each word I said, and showed a brotherly affection in his manner towards me. He had heard that we were leaving Turkey on the morrow to return to England, and expressed deep sorrow upon that account. Among a number of most bare-faced compliments addressed to me he made the rather strange remark that my wife possessed a musical and pleasant voice, and not a harsh one like the other English ladies who from time to time had come to look at Turkish women. Her manner was not domineering and she did not ask a lot of questions. The ladies were quite sad about her going. He, too, was sad to think of parting with so tough and staunch an adversary as myself. We should, he hoped, return and make our home with Turks for good.

"Why are you coming into town this morning?" he asked with some appearance of solicitude. "Preparatory to so long a journey, you should have stayed at home and rested in the house and garden."

I told him I was going to Stamboul in order to keep an appointment which a friend had kindly made for me, to see the Minister of the Interior at eleven o'clock.

"And what are you going to say to His Excellency?" he demanded in the ironical tone which Liberals invariably used when mentioning a light of Unionism.

I was going, first of all, to say good-bye; but the friend who had arranged the interview insisted on my making known the views which I had formed about reforms in Turkey, which happened, by good luck, to be his own.

"And what are they?" he inquired. "We have argued up and down, but I have never heard them."

The state of Turkey—judging from the region of the capital and such of the provinces as I knew intimately—appeared to me extraordinarily hopeful, if only Turks had not such large ideas. The Turks were proud. Their pride, when it rang true—as, for example in resistance to their foreign enemies—was admirable; but in the matters of internal government, improvements and reforms, it sometimes wore the look of megalomania, a disease. They conceived huge projects, gratifying to their pride as a great nation, forgetting —so it struck me—that those projects must be forced on the acceptance of some millions of unknown and unregarded individuals, who might object to schemes of which they did not understand one word or see the aim. The people simply gaped and wondered; they could not collaborate. The beginning of all true reform, in my opinion, must be in a small district in a small way—in hundreds of such districts, simultaneously if possible; if not, in one. One little district, working for improvement, the villages

## Chapter XXII: Farewells

and towns performing each its part, and every man aware of what the purpose was, would, in the present state of feeling of the Turkish people, set others going. It would be worth all the schemes of all the Ministries, for it would rouse enthusiasm in the populace which theoretic schemes did not.

"I quite agree with you," he answered seriously. "I myself have often thought what grand results could be obtained by anyone who would devote his whole attention to a little district for ten years. Many of us have long realised the truth of what you say. Every governor of a province, who has worked upon those lines, has met success. The trouble hitherto has been the lack of sequence, of a general scheme. The successor of a great reformer has let things relapse. The schemes which you deride have this advantage: that they do make progress law, and do ensure a measure of consistency at least in the ideals and aims of government. Do you know why many of us—I myself, for instance—seeing what you see, have not gone down into some province and improved it? Simply because they gave us no security. Supposing that I left the capital, I knew for certain that the moment that my back was turned my enemies would work up some intrigue against me. Not only should I lose what influence I had possessed at court, but should ere long be superseded in my government, my work destroyed. Though things are better now the government is far from settled, and a change of government would mean a man's removal, without recompense, from the province he had just begun to study and to raise. There is another hardships and the deprivations of provincial life. Such work as you suggest would have to be conducted without interruption for at least ten years. My wife will not go with me; therefore I give up the project, sooner than assume the cares of further matrimony. Give the Minister your views, by all means! It may do some good. He has both power and energy." My companion uttered the last sentence with an air of generosity, as who would say: "To give the Devil his due!"

Like everybody else who comes to town from country places where the roads are deep in dust or mud, according to the season, I had my boots cleaned instantly on my arrival at the Bridge. I then put up my parasol—the sun was blazing—and sauntered over to Stamboul, watching the stir of shipping on the Golden Horn, the colours of the passing crowd, quite sad to think that I was strolling there for the last time, until I came into the quarter of the Turkish booksellers, where I spent the period of waiting happily, though always with the feeling of the last time.

Punctually at eleven o'clock I passed between the sentries at the gate of the Sublime Porte and made my way to the Ministry of the Interior. The Sublime Porte! What kind of vision do the words evoke for people who have never seen the modern building. The reality is a long wall with iron railings up above it and two gates, admitting to a yard before a long and lofty structure full of windows like a barracks, the central part whereof is now a fire-stained ruin, with grass growing in the yard before it, and within. In the two wings, at one end of this blackened desolation is the Grand Vizierate, at the other the Foreign Office, the Interior, and other Ministries. The portions which remain in use are so extensive, and offer so bewildering a labyrinth of stairs and corridors, that the humble suitor gasps to think of what the intricacies of the building must have been before the fire destroyed two-thirds of it. It was pleasant, remembering my feelings of five months before, soon after my arrival in Constantinople, when I had strayed among those corridors, having an appointment but very nearly hopeless of direction through my lack of Turkish, to find myself at ease in talk with guards and ushers, my questions understood and promptly answered. On one previous occasion of my going there, on emerging from a Minister's reception room I had taken the wrong turning and, having forgotten the Turkish word for "out of doors" (dishariya) had to perform the pantomime of diving from an upper window in order to explain my predicament to a small crowd of soldiers who only gaped at words of Arabic, French, German, and Italian. On this occasion I was shown at once into the ante-chamber of the Minister, where the secretary, after shaking hands, conducted me at once into the presence of the Minister himself.

The view from the tall windows of his salon— the old palace with its quaint kiosks and gardens sloping to the sea, and then the Bosphorus, as blue as cornflowers, with all the pageant of its shipping, winding among the many-coloured towns and hills—has not its equal, I imagine, in the world. Tala'at Bey asked what I had to say; and, having heard me kindly to an end, remarked:

"We have all that in mind. Remember that the Powers, by asking for reforms at all points simultaneously and instantly, oblige us to produce those big schemes you dislike. But all the while good work is going on; though everybody must admit that it is under difficulties."

He then told me that the Turkish army was advancing to the Enos-Midia line, no further, and, after some general conversation on the subject of Bulgaria's plight, I took my leave. I then went on to call upon another Minister, whose office was across the road and up some steps. There I was kept waiting half an hour, quite unintentionally as it afterwards transpired. For, on my being shown at last into the great man's room, he started up and cried:

"What! Is it you? How ever long then have I kept you waiting!"

My card was in his hand; but it had carried nothing to his understanding, because, though we had met and talked a dozen times, he had never had an inkling of my name, beyond the fact that it began with something like Mahmud. When I said that I had just heard that the army was advancing to the Enos-Midia line he gave a shrug and hinted that the army, once in motion, would not easily be stopped, at any rate by orders from Stamboul.

On reaching home I found that Misket Hanum had received a visit which had greatly agitated her.

A Levantine gentleman, who knew her only slightly as a European, being in the neighbourhood, had called upon her. He was one of many who had fled the country in October, fearing massacre, and had only lately summoned courage to return. He asked her whether she had not been greatly frightened in the bad days of the war.

"Frightened! Of what?" she asked.

Of the fanaticism of the Turks. Of course it was well known that everyone had gone away who could contrive to do so. How had she endured the strain of daily terror? What had she done? Misket Hanum then informed him plainly that she loved the Turks and hated their traducers. What had she done? She had nursed the wounded; had worked for the poor, ill-clad, starving soldiers; she had done her best to comfort the poor, anxious women. And she had met with kindness, courtesy, and touching gratitude. There had never been the slightest danger; there was no fanaticism.

"What! You never mean to say you're a pro-Turk!" cried the Levantine, who, as a British subject, spoke English always in his pride of race.

Misket Hanum asked him whether in all the years that he had lived in Turkey he had ever suffered anything from any Turk. He could not say he had. What then had he been so afraid of that he ran away? The visitor explained that, to his thinking, the Turks were only tolerant of "us Europeans" through fear of our protecting governments. When all Europe fell on them, it had seemed to him a certainty that they would massacre. Misket Hanum's indignation made her almost speechless. In the end (if I remember rightly) she referred to me—an Englishman then staying in her house who, if he heard him talking thus about the Turks, would have his blood (or something of that kind); upon which awful intimation he departed, as Misket Hanum told us later, "like a man who does not know the earth from sky." But the shock of meeting such a person made her downright ill.

However, in the morning, she appeared herself again, and nothing would dissuade her from escorting us on board our steamer.

As we left the house to walk up to the railway-station, our luggage having gone before, a heavy splash of water close behind me made me jump. Turning, I saw the Greek maid grinning, holding upside down an empty jug. Cry of "Insh Allah!" came from the Turkish ladies looking on. "It is to make you both come back!" said Misket Hanum. "If water is poured out between you and the house you leave, you are bound to return to it sooner or later. It is well-known."

The Turkish ladies went no further than the garden gate where long farewells were said; and then we two, with Misket Hanum, habited as Europeans, wandered out into the world.

Two hours before the sun set, we were standing on the deck of a great steamer, high above the quay of Ghalata. We had just said good-bye to the last of our friends—a Turkish youth who had had the news of our departure only that same morning in a letter from his sister, and on the news had ridden from his farm in the interior to Beykoz on the Bosphorus, where he could get a steamer, arriving only just in time, at the last minute, after our other friends had left the ship. He was now standing with them in the crowd below, waving his handkerchief. A tug at bow and stern was pulling out the great ship, broadside on, into the open strait. Slowly, almost imperceptibly, the quay receded. The crowd piled up on it became a mist, the volleys of farewells no longer audible; only the flutter of the handkerchiefs could be distinguished. That also vanished, and the city claimed our eyes. The tugs cast off, the steamer throbbed to life. The glorious vista of the Golden Horn, the old palace and the lighthouse, the Mosque of Sultan Ahmed slipped away, to be restored to us far out at sea in one vast panorama with the hills of Asia. We sat on deck and watched it till the sun sank.

www.ingramcontent.com/pod-product-compliance
Lightning Source LLC
Chambersburg PA
CBHW012004090526
44590CB00026B/3874